REVEALED!

SMARTSELLING STRATEGIES

SECOND EDITION

EDDY MINDLIN

Revealed!
SmartSelling Strategies
Second Edition
by Eddy Mindlin

Copyright © 2017 Eddy Mindlin

ISBN-13:978-1973770213
ISBN-10:1973770210

Second Edition

Contents

Introduction to the
Second Edition

WHEN I PUBLISHED THE first edition of *Revealed!* in 2013, it was not my intention to write a second edition. My goal was to share the methodology that had helped me realize a significant level of success as a sales professional, while also achieving the work/family/life balance that I wanted for my life.

Based on the feedback and letters I received from readers, many of them were able to implement some of my systems and reach the goals that were important to them.

At about the same time I wrote *Revealed!* I began investing more of my time in coaching other sales professionals. This has given me the opportunity to talk with many men and women in different fields, who sell a variety of products and services. Some of this coaching has been in person, in conversations after a presentation, or with those who purchased my video training program.

It became clear to me that most sales training programs that were being marketed focused on technology, such as using email blasts. While this strategy can lead to some initial success, it forces the salesperson who chooses this method for growing their business to be constantly mass marketing, at the expense of personal calls and building long-term business relationships that can become mutually profitable.

In this second edition of *Revealed!* I address this dilemma, and suggest some ways that a new or experienced salesperson can combine the power of today's technology with the "old school" focus on relationships that lead to consistent repeat business.

Most of the information in this updated edition was taken from recordings of my live presentations and video training program. I love speaking with groups of sales professionals, and I hope that the passion I have comes through in these pages.

I've also added new chapters specifically for salespeople who work online, in retail, or as inside sales team members, primarily helping their customers on the telephone. Those of you who work in these environments will find that the relationship-building strategies used by someone who is out in the field calling on clients are equally important for inside salespeople.

I hope that you find this information to be helpful in your career as a sales professional, as well as interesting and enjoyable to read. At the end of the book I have some suggestions for next steps if you'd like to talk with me personally. One of my greatest joys as a sales coach is the time I spend with other salespeople. I hope we have the opportunity to meet in the future.

To Your Success!

Eddy

Confidence and enthusiasm are the greatest sales producers in any kind of economy.

O. B. Smith

Athletes need to enjoy their training. They don't enjoy going down to the track with a coach making them do repetitions until they're exhausted. From enjoyment comes the will to win.

Arthur Lydiard

1. What is The Goal?

On the Road to Sales Success: Passion, Fun, and Profit

MY GOAL FOR WRITING this book for you is very simple: to help you design a system of being organized in order to create passion, fun, and profit for yourself in your sales business. After thirty-five successful years in sales, my passion is to inspire and help you make your career in sales fun and profitable. Anyone involved in sales must have goals, and we all know how important those goals are in achieving success. I have put my thirty-five years of experience into this book to help you create your own attainable goals and to achieve success in sales. I love working with people, and that's why part of my work is being a sales coach. In my sales coaching, including both individual and corporate consulting, as well as coaching webinars, I share and explain the art of being a salesperson, which I have fine-tuned over the course of my sales career in the flooring industry.

There is an art to being an accomplished and successful salesperson. In this book, and in my webinars and personal trainings, I share with you my personal experience and guide you in creating your own systems for finding your clients and developing long-term relationships, for organizing your daily schedule, and following up on long-term sales and planning for the future. Not only will you have more fun, but you will feel more relaxed. Our goal together is to make your sales system fun and profitable.

Much of what you will discover in this book is how to fine-tune the art of being a successful salesperson. I will help you land in the top five to ten percent in your industry. It's absolutely essential for every salesperson to know a lot about the products and services they sell. Most salespeople are taught about the products they sell, but are not taught how to be a great salesperson. When I began my career in sales, I was sent to visit carpet mills to learn the process of making flooring. But no one ever taught me how to be a successful salesperson. I struggled every day with learning how to be the best salesperson possible. You don't need to struggle, because in this book you will learn a lot from my personal experience. I encourage you to adapt what you learn from this book to your own style and personalized systems for relationships, organizing, and closing sales. Success will soon follow.

Think about the professional athletes who are the best in the world. They all have a coach, no matter their level of success. The coach serves as a trainer, an advocate, and confidant for these stars. They are not embarrassed to have a coach; it's simply part of their success and their stardom. They never want to stop improving and learning. They also know that on their own they can't see what they need to do to improve. Athletes and salespeople need a coach who can see what the athlete or sales-person can't see. A good coach can spot the things the person needs to work on and keep them from falling into bad habits. That is why the best athletes and salespeople have ongoing coaching. These people want to be the best, and they understand how beneficial a coach is to their success.

I invite you to join me on a journey to becoming a more successful salesperson and growing in your personal and professional life, while enjoying the process of sales, having fun with your clients, and reaping the profits of your hard work and very successful sales systems.

> Abundance mentality vs. scarcity mentality:
> Many salespeople think there are very few
> possibilities. The best salespeople know
> there are always more prospects. Remember
> that numerous opportunities await you.

Almost thirty years ago Stephen Covey wrote a powerful book called *The 7 Habits of Highly Effective People*. In it he suggested some common traits characteristic of the most successful people in all fields. One of those seven habits is, "Begin with the end in mind."

What he meant by that phrase is crucial to success: know where you're going. Be clear on your goal as you begin a project, so that you will know when you get there.

As simple as this sounds, most of us forget to do it. Instead, we get an idea for our business and immediately dive in, going "full speed ahead." We hear a speaker, read a book, or watch one of our peers and decide to go in a new direction, often with very little thought to where it might lead, or whether it is taking us in the direction of our goals at all.

As you start reading this book, designed to help you be more successful as a sales professional, I want to help you avoid the trap of losing sight of your goals. So before we talk about techniques, let's review exactly what an effective salesperson does.

Successful people set long-term goals, and they know that these aims are merely the result of short-term habits that they need to engage in every day. These healthy habits shouldn't be something you do; they should be something you embody.

Knowing what an effective salesperson does and knowing where you are going and how you will get there—having a step-by-step plan to be organized—are essential when setting out to achieve success in sales. This chapter covers the first things you need to know and need to do to attain your desired results as you head toward finalizing a sale, beginning with finding your clients.

An effective salesperson—one who produces out-standing results—will carry out each step in the process from meeting a potential client to closing the sale with equal determination and intention. It's also important to be persistent. Here are some of the steps that I have found to be almost universal among successful salespeople:

- Meet someone in person and tell them what you do.
- Put the potential client's name and contact information in your database and keep your database current.
- As appropriate, include the project name and the stage of every project.
- Assign a follow-up date to each project.
- Find out about additional projects that may use your products.
- Find out when decisions will be made and note the date.
- Follow up on that date.
- Take the appropriate action. If your client gives you a "yes" to take it to the next step, make an appointment and present your products.
- If a project is still in a planning stage, find out when your client would like you to follow up next. Then, when you contact your client, remind them that you are contacting them at this time because they asked you to.

Pro-athletes need coaches because "they can't see what they are doing wrong" and the coaches show them how they can improve, and they provide constant reminders. People in our society today often feel that if they ask for help, they are perceived as weak. The opposite is true. The most successful people all have coaches!

Finding Your Clients

To be an effective and successful salesperson, the first step in your strategic plan is finding your clients. You can't go anywhere without a client—you need a client to make a sale. In sales, the formula for a winning performance is whom you know and who knows you.

As you build your database, it's important to stay in touch with everyone so they remember you and what you sell. Stay in touch after your first call. Up to eighty percent of salespeople quit after the first call. That's when I'm just getting started! At the same time, be sensitive to proper timing and your client's preferences about how often they want to be contacted. Find out whether they prefer to be contacted in person, or by phone, email, or text. Use your personal skills to expand this list of active contacts. They represent your current and future projects.

A brilliant salesperson is on constant alert for referrals. Telling people "I want your help" makes them feel part of what you do, and they will take ownership and responsibility in helping you. One example that was beneficial to me was my wife helping me sell several projects by suggesting that I call companies she had worked with. I have received nice letters of recommendation from these clients.

Throughout this book you will find many suggestions for ways to identify new sources of business. The number of new people you meet each week, follow-up conversations with existing contacts, and referrals that lead to new clients are important metrics for setting goals.

So, What Are Your Goals?

You may already have targets given to you by a sales manager or the owner of your company. If that is the case, then developing your plan to achieve those target numbers is the next step.

If you manage your own sales business, identifying the key performance indicators that drive your business should be your focus. How many calls do you make to get an appointment? How many appointments does it take to have the opportunity to prepare a proposal? What is your closing date once you present your product or service?

While sales is definitely a "people" business based on relationships, it is also a "numbers" business. Those who are the most successful understand this and manage their business by the numbers. Before jumping into the following chapters, please take some time to think about your goals for your business, as well as other areas of your life, such as health, family, or personal development.

Realizing that you are responsible for what happens next in your life is both frightening and exciting. Successful people invest an immense amount of time on a daily basis to develop a growth mindset, acquire new knowledge, learn new skills, and change their perception so that it can benefit their lives.

SmartSelling Strategies: What is the Goal?

- Think about the professional athletes who are the best in the world. They all have a coach, no matter their level of success. The coach serves as a trainer, an advocate, and confidant for these stars. They are not embarrassed to have a coach, it's simply part of their success and their stardom.
- Knowing what an effective salesperson does and knowing where you are going and how you will get there—having a step-by-step plan to be organized—are essential when setting out to achieve success in sales.
- To be an effective and successful salesperson, the first step in your strategic plan is finding your clients.
- While sales is definitely a "people" business based on relationships, it is also a "numbers" business. Those who are the most successful understand this and manage their business by the numbers.

*Success seems to be connected
with action. Successful people keep
moving. They make mistakes, but
they never quit.*

Conrad Hilton

*Make sure your worst enemy
doesn't live between your own
two ears.*

Laird Hamilton

2. Organization and Time Management

BUILDING YOUR CLIENT BASE is something like keeping track of a snowball that will grow and grow. But you must be organized to manage this snowball as it grows. When you start in your sales career or you begin a new job as a salesperson, you'll have just a few clients. One goal will be to acquire more clients. The process works like a snowball. The number of clients starts small and it keeps rolling, getting bigger and bigger. You must be organized to keep track of all this. If you aren't organized and you reach a hundred clients, or two hundred, it could become chaos and you will lose sales. It's essential to have a system to manage clients and projects and to know what is needed next for each of them, and when it is needed. Your survival in sales depends on being organized and developing good organizational skills.

Tracking projects is important to your success. A project-driven approach means that you know approximately when your client will be in the market for what you sell. Tracking the project means staying in contact with the client and also asking when they will start to make a decision on their purchase. Try to be face to face with your client at that time. Build this information into your system.

The Tube

A primary tool I use for being organized in my sales process is what I call "the tube." This is a mental or psychological tool. Just imagine a tube. It can be a cylinder of any kind that goes on for maybe a mile. Create a picture of this tube in your mind and constantly hold the image of the tube in your brain, with information about the clients and the projects you're working on. Visualize these clients or projects moving through the tube to completion and then going out the end of the tube. Once a project reaches completion, that's an order, and you get your commission check. It's amazing how your visualization will help keep your projects moving toward completion. Sometimes a project will work itself part way through, and then stop at a particular point. It might be another two months before you can follow up or find out why that happened. Or perhaps the client informs you that they are not quite ready to buy. It's inevitable that some projects will drop out somewhere along the way. But all the projects that you are working on are at some stage advancing through this tube.

When I was twenty-two years old and out of college, I was living in Dallas and joined a company that was selling advertising space in a magazine called *Foodservice News*. The magazine was delivered free to restaurant owners. My boss was not the friendliest person in the world, but he did teach me this one thing—the tube. This concept of the tube has helped me every day in my sales career. It was also a lesson for me that you can learn from any type of person—you never know where you'll learn something that will help you in sales. This man told me to visualize this tube, and I have always remembered it.

Sometimes you will lose a project or a client. Perhaps the client doesn't have the money or they're no longer interested; many things may happen. But it's a great visual tool for you to think about projects going through the tube. Because sales is a numbers game, the more potential clients and company businesses you have in the tube, the better it is. Be organized to keep track of all those people and their sales activity, and know the right time to follow up with them.

It is helpful psychologically to think about this tube. It is reassuring to know you are making progress on many projects that will turn into orders for you. It feels good to be organized, to know what you need to do tomorrow or next week. It has helped me immensely to calm down and be more relaxed in sales, because I know I have possible orders in the tube. When you visualize your projects in the tube on a daily basis, it's likely that you will also benefit.

Two-tier Filing System

What about all the notes and papers scattered across your desk? I have a two-tier file system on my desk, which I will explain. One of the advantages of working with me as a consultant in the sales process is that I will explain to you how I do things. But in no way will I try to push that on you. I will give you an idea, and then together we'll come up with a plan specifically designed for you. I use a manual filing system, but there are options for project management using digital management and software systems. Three digital systems (CRM, Client Relationship Management Software) include such programs as ACT!, Sales Force, and SharpSpring.

On my desk I have two files that are stacked one on top of the other. Current projects are in the top file. I begin by writing all client information on a piece of paper, whether it's a client's name or a specific project. I keep complete notes in order to be organized. The notes may also be in a file in a computer. In my system, in the upper-right-hand corner of each page there is a follow-up date. It could be next week, next month, or next year. If something is due to happen in the current month, it is put in the top file. If it's something scheduled to happen next month or ten months from now or two years from now, it goes in the bottom file. So the two files are arranged according to a timeframe. Again, the top file includes only projects that will happen or require follow-up in the current month. At the end of every week, I review all the notes in the top file. This is where the funnel comes in—I'm narrowing down and figuring out which projects I will work on in the next week and current month; I'm planning and organizing. Any notes in the bottom file refer to projects that are scheduled for follow-up in future months. At the end of each month, every project in the bottom file is reviewed and moved to the top file if follow-up is scheduled for the coming month.

One approach to the pile of notes is to decide how many projects you can follow up on in the coming week. It might only be half of them that you can manage. I'll put half in my "weekly to-do file," which contains a paper for each day of the week. This way it is easy to see how many calls I have on any one day. You might set up a new page for each day and note those phone calls and appointments you need to schedule. Again, this top file is the urgent projects, within the week or month, and the bottom file is for projects to follow up on in the next month or later.

For immediate projects, check the top file every week. Use the notes to prioritize what's going to happen next. If it's the end of the month, but follow-up is not for three weeks, the project remains in the top file, but constantly narrow down each day or each week. Once you make the phone calls and see the clients, schedule another follow-up with them. Often a client will say that they would like to meet again in a couple of months to talk more about your products or services. Remember to change the follow-up date on your notes for that client and leave the file in whichever tier is appropriate for the revised follow-up date. Following up at the right time is essential to keep projects moving. This simple approach of a two-tier system will make organizing easy and fun. You will make more sales and more money as you become more organized and are able to track many clients and projects.

Organization and follow-up are so critical. It's often most efficient to check your files at night or on the weekends, as opposed to normal business hours, because you need to be seeing your clients and working with them during business hours. If you do your planning in the evening, phone calls won't interrupt you, so take ample time to plan at night or on the weekends. Many salespeople are totally the opposite. Whether they work out of their house or in an office, they'll go into the office at eight o'clock and get a cup of coffee, and then think about what they're going to do; they're already behind at that point. In order to be the best salesperson, when you have planned ahead you will know when you begin your day exactly what you will be doing.

> Rely on yourself: never
> complain or make excuses.

It feels good to be organized—you will even sleep better when you are well organized. Knowing that you have projects to work on six months from now is a good feeling. Many salespeople get very anxious, wondering what they will be working on in the coming months. If you use this system or a similar system, you will always have projects to work on.

Sales can be stressful, as is the case for a lot of other professions. We all get stressed out about all kinds of things. If you are feeling nervous, it comes across to your clients, and that's not something you want to project. Being organized will help you be calm and will take away much of your stress.

Tracking Your Projects

Keeping track of all clients and all projects is highly important. When I'm coaching a client, one of the first things I'll ask is for them to tell me about the projects they're working on. Usually they mention the number of active projects they have. They might mention the name of one or two. But if I ask for the file on a specific project, often they tell me they are not sure where the file is. Then I know there's a problem that I can help with.

If your sales manager requests information, or if you own your own company, you need to always be able to quickly locate the file for any specific project or person. The client may call you, or you may remember that you need to call the person. When you are contacted by a client you must respond in a short time, preferably during the same day.

Being organized keeps you from scrambling, and you know what you will work on next. There's no need to scramble to figure out what to do next or whom to call next. You might go to see a client who doesn't need a particular product or service you are presenting. But when you ask when your client might need what you are selling, the client may suggest that you follow up with them at a future date, perhaps even in a year. Many salespeople won't do that follow-up—in fact, the majority won't do it. But when that year comes around, you have something to work on. And, you're following up with that person when they asked you to. When you do what the client asks, the client will begin to trust you. That's very strategic in helping your client base grow.

Daily Schedule

It's important to maintain a schedule for your daily phone calls and your face-to-face business. Sales is exciting because every day you will be doing different things and your priorities will be constantly changing. If every day you have five to ten phone calls to make, they will be noted in your weekly to-do folder. For me, usually five or ten phone calls in a day is plenty, along with meetings to see people at their offices. And you have a variety of in-office work and out-of-office work. If you over-schedule yourself, you won't be as effective and efficient as you could otherwise be. On any given day, it's not really important how many people you see. The quality of each face-to-face sales call is much more important than the quantity.

Leave Time for the Unexpected

Leave time for the unexpected. Unexpected requests or issues will come up in any business. Avoid over-scheduling yourself with too many phone calls and clients to see in one day. Set yourself up to be a winner, and leave time for the unexpected, such as when a client calls with an urgent need.

Continually reprioritize the tasks that you need to do every day. You will be prepared for unexpected situations that come up as you learn how to reprioritize your day and your week. When somebody calls you needing some product or service right away and asking you to show up, you will be able to allow time for that. If you take care of the request on the same day, or the next at the latest, the odds are good you will get an order. It may be most efficient to cancel an appointment and reschedule it for later, in order to take care of the person needing immediate assistance. So always be prepared to reprioritize to handle urgent requests from your customers. These are some of the techniques I use: put a star next to something that's important on a daily call sheet; list immediate tasks using bold letters; highlight urgent tasks. If some-body calls unexpectedly and needs something, put that in capital letters. Create a system that works for you to be highly organized.

Prioritizing Your Clients: the A-B-C List

Maintaining an **A-B-C** list of clients, prioritizing clients according to their business with you, will help you know where to direct your attention. You will have **A** clients, **B** clients, and **C** clients, the **A** clients being the most im-portant in terms of the business they bring you. Review your **A** clients every week. For example, in my business I have about twenty-five **A** clients. These are the people I make my living from because of their large amount of business. We respect and trust each other.

Always work on bringing the **B** and **C** clients up to the **A** level, to be more important. But the reality is that it always comes down to the 80-20 rule. If you have a hundred clients or a hundred prospects, twenty of them will be the most critical for you, and that's where you will make your living. Keep your **A-B-C** list in a computer and know where everybody stands: how you rate them. Regardless of where they are, treat all clients the same. But plan to spend more time and effort on the **A** clients.

Stay focused and active with each **A** client even though they might not be your biggest client. The **A** client is someone you get along with well, and they get along with you. You share a mutual respect; you like each other and you work well together. If you have several clients who are smaller clients, but they're very important to you, they may be rated as **A** clients.

All salespeople have a variety of clients. Years ago one of the most important things a sales manager told me was to remember the three letters M-I-X, which of course spell *mix*. A mix of clients creates a balanced business. Some big clients, some medium-sized clients, and some small clients all together will provide a stable sales business. Smaller clients, the **B** and **C** clients, are easier to work with than the huge clients; there is usually less competition, so working with those can be beneficial. With the **A** clients, you will have a nice business relationship regardless of the amount of business, but often they are providing most of your income.

It's more difficult to get new clients than it is to retain the clients you already have. Whether you have ten clients or a hundred clients, it's important not to lose any of them. Yes, it's inevitable that you will lose a few, and for many different reasons. But if you lose a small percentage each year, as opposed to a large percentage, the retention of clients goes a long way. It takes ongoing effort, many phone calls and emails, and many site visits face to face to get a new client. Because a lot of energy is required to get a new client and start all over again, take good care of the clients you have.

Plan on spending a lot of time with your **A** clients, because it is difficult to replace them. Work hard for them; it's worth the extra effort to "baby" them. It's important to always be there for the **A** clients, which may mean frequently reprioritizing your schedule to accommodate them. Tell those **A** clients that they are one of your most important clients. Be authentic when you tell them that they are an **A** client, in the top tier of your client relationships. You might say to a client: "Here's how I run my business: I have **A** clients, **B** clients, and **C** clients, and you're a nice-size client, and you are on my **A**-list because you are very important to me. I like the way you treat me and I think you appreciate the way I treat you. We have a nice business relationship." People appreciate hearing this from you, so verbalize this with your clients.

Organization equals success and fun. To be successful you must be organized. There is no other way to do it. It's simple: to be a great salesperson, being highly organized is essential. And having fun with what you're doing is important, too. Sales will be more fun when you're organized, because you always know what to do next with each customer. On the other hand, disorganization equals frustration and burnout. Your job will be so much harder if you're disorganized: you're getting ready to go see a client, but you cannot find the file; you need to call them, but you don't know where their phone number is. It's easy to avoid the aggravation of chaos when you develop good systems to be organized.

Learn from other people: what you see them do and what you hear them say. Read books and trade journals to make yourself a better person.

I remember when I was starting my own sales agency in 1988. My database was in a three-ring binder, and I tried my best to have the **A** clients on a couple of pages and the **B**s on a couple pages, but it got overwhelming. I contacted a technical person to help me with my database. I provided the categories of people I called on and the types of projects I worked on, and the computer person created a database for me. I can now easily find my clients and any phone number I need. It's easy to become overwhelmed if you're disorganized, and that leads to failure. When you're overwhelmed, you don't know what to do next. When you are organized, your business will grow.

As your client base expands—remember the snowball effect—it's essential to know who all those people are, and what all those projects are about. Organization equals success. Don't lose projects because you're disorganized. I've had this happen in the past, but it doesn't happen very often now because I am highly organized. Also, your clients know how well organized you are. When they ask you to get some information for them and you do it quickly, they will realize that you are organized. Clients want to work with organized people. They will respect you for being the kind of person they want to work with.

Strive to improve your organization. It might be helpful to hire a consultant like myself to help you get organized. Ask your friends for help, ask any of your peers for help, and people will usually be honest with you and give you ideas. Visit my website for an overview of the consulting services and webinars I offer, which can help you with your organizational skills.

Taking Breaks

Take breaks each day. Sometimes salespeople try to impress others by mentioning how many hours they worked in a day, how many people they visited, or how many hours they spent in the office. It really doesn't matter, because what is important is the quality of each sales call and how well you serve your clients. You will avoid becoming overwhelmed by taking breaks each day. Get up from your desk. Or, if you're planning to see five or ten people in a day, take a couple of minutes and enjoy a short walk. It's amazing how walking will calm down your brain, and clients will appreciate how calm you are. Working out and exercising are also helpful. Try to work out regularly; it's great for your body, great for your brain, and it makes you a better salesperson—you're calm, you're relaxed, you're in good shape. You will have more energy to be a really top-notch salesperson.

SMARTSELLING STRATEGIES: ORGANIZATION AND TIME MANAGEMENT

- A primary goal in sales is to meet new clients and build your client base.
- Make time to keep your client database current.
- Your system of being organized must ensure that you can easily find each client: their contact information and their projects.
- Know your clients: keep an A-B-C list, the A clients being your best clients, and always strive to move the Bs to A and the Cs to B. Focus on the A clients.
- A visualization technique such as "the tube" will help keep projects moving forward in your mind until they are complete.

- A two-tier filing system is a simple way to track projects that require your attention in the current week or month, and to be timely with following up on projects in the next few months or further out in the year.
- Always keep written notes when you meet with any client. Include a follow-up date on each note.
- Be realistic about how many projects you can follow up in a week.
- Follow up on the date that you committed to with your client and in your notes.
- Being organized is key to reducing stress and being relaxed when you meet clients.
- Keep a daily and weekly appointment schedule, and have it with you when you go out on calls.
- Remember to always allow time for the unexpected.
- Learn how to reprioritize your daily schedule when it is necessary to attend to something immediately.
- Take breaks every day so that you are refreshed and relaxed.

The Art of Getting Along: depends about ninety-eight percent on your own behavior.

Hugh M. Cunningham

Seek opportunities to show you care. The smallest gestures often make the biggest difference.

John Wooden

3. Sales Psychology

Understand Yourself First

I⊤'s IMPORTANT TO UNDERSTAND your own psychology. Most people don't try to understand themselves and what drives their own behavior. How many people look in the mirror with a pad of paper and say, "I am good at this," "I am not so good at this"? We all have strengths and weaknesses; it doesn't mean you're a bad person if you have weaknesses. You will be helping yourself if you take the time to write a list of your strengths and weaknesses. Get friends to help you with this process by asking them to share their observations. Then you know what to work on. What is it that makes you tick, what do you like, what turns you off?

The important thing about your own psychology, knowing how you "work," is that you need to adapt to your client. Your client is not going to change—that's not your goal at all. Your goal in understanding sales psychology is to learn about yourself and then to learn about your clients. Each client will be different. You need to know how to adapt to their style and how they want to work with you.

Work on yourself.
Nobody can change others!

It's fun to learn about yourself, your own psychology, and it's fun to learn about each client. If you treat every client as the same type of person, you will have issues in your sales career. Be attentive and be willing to work on yourself. Then you will be able to quickly size-up a client and figure out what kind of personality they are. Are they the kind of person who likes to chat? Are they a very quiet person, or are they a loud person or a soft talker? Do they want to know all the details about your product, or are they the kind of person who just wants a quick overview, then they want you to get out of the way? Try to understand these dynamics with each client.

Be honest about yourself. That's difficult for anybody to do; it was hard for me to do. I've had to work on the tone of my voice, how much I talk, how loud I talk. My nature is to talk loudly, but I know that if I'm talking too loudly it could be a turn-off to the client. Also, the tone of your voice and how loud you speak can determine how well a person listens to you. When you speak more softly, people listen more attentively. Vary your voice. Those behaviors that you can adjust are important for your sales success. The last person someone wants to listen to or work with is someone who speaks in a monotone: someone who has the same tone of voice for twenty minutes when giving a presentation. Think about these behaviors, and be willing and honest to work on yourself.

You Can't Change Your Clients

You are part psychologist if you are a salesperson. You will be dealing with many types of people. If a client has five people involved in the decision-making process regarding your service or product, there will be interaction among those five people. They may not get along among themselves. Each person will have a unique psychology, and subtle interactions will go on. Work to understand the clients better. It's so important. Clients will not change so they are more fun to work with or they spend more time with you; you can't ask them to change.

You must be the one to change and adapt to your clients. You will have easy, comfortable relationships with some clients, no issues, and they'll have no issue with you. From day one you'll start talking together and you will become good business friends and have a satisfying business relationship. It's helpful to mesh with your client by finding familiar topics and common interests to talk about; you will do a lot better with the client.

Is the client paying attention to you? Be aware of this. I've observed many different salespeople and coaching clients over my career and have seen that they are often not aware when they're talking or giving a presentation that the client or audience is not listening. They might be looking at their phones or chatting with each other during the presentation—that's not a good sign. Are you dragging on your conversation too long? Is your presentation too long? Do you need to get to the point more quickly? I never had this issue because I get right to the point. The client knows what I'm there for; I show them the product or service, and if they want me to continue to stay, I will. Otherwise, I leave because I know they've got other things to do, which they appreciate.

The Art of Listening

Watch the client's facial and body movements. These are telling signs of their interest in what you are saying. Are you talking too much? Try to listen twice as much as you talk. There's no problem having some silence in a conversation, especially when the client needs to think about something, or when you're giving a talk and you stop speaking for five seconds. If you stop for a few seconds, the client has time to think about what you've said. These pauses are very important. Remember to always put on your "psychologist hat." And as mentioned earlier, taking notes during a conversation shows the client that you are interested in what they are saying.

Do you need to slow down? I've learned in my sales career that I need to take some deep breaths every now and then. I have observed that many salespeople are that way. Take a few deep breaths occasionally. It shows that you're working on being calm and paying attention to the client.

Are you giving your client time to speak until they're finished, without interrupting? This is very important in sales psychology. If you interrupt your client, they may be upset with you or stop talking. Don't interrupt your client; practice the art of listening.

How Your Clients See You

Be aware of how you come across to your clients. What do you need to do to change? Think about the key behaviors you need to change to get along better with your clients, and to help them be at ease with you. Work on these aspects of yourself as it relates to sales psychology. The reality with salespeople is that many of us don't work on ourselves; we won't do it on our own. This is a common theme in my webinars and when I work as a coach. If you learn to monitor your own behavior when you are with clients, you will be more successful and a step ahead of your competition. Give yourself a little prompt by writing down what you want to work on or improve.

Clients are always judging you, whether you are aware of it, or not. They are forming opinions about you, just like you have opinions about them. For example, if someone fails to show up for an appointment, you wonder what's going on, and then you have an opinion about that person. But you need to find out why they were late. People, in their personal lives, perhaps in their family, run into all kinds of problems, which can reflect on how they behave with you. Be careful not to take it personally, because maybe they're just having a bad day or they're going through a difficult period in their life.

Being aware of how you relate to clients is sales psychology. Be friendly and show that you have the interest of the client at heart. Usually you need to see a client five times face to face before they will begin to trust you. Think about how it would be for yourself, if you were planning to buy a big-ticket item. You don't know if the salesperson will come back. It takes time to trust that person. In a similar way, the person you're working with, the buyer or the purchasing manager at the firm, doesn't know you. When you meet for the first time, and you're trying to sell a thousand-dollar or a fifty-thousand-dollar product—these are big-ticket items—the client wants to have trust in you. Most salespeople quit after the first or second sales call if they haven't obtained that purchase order. The client will begin to trust you when you are persistent, and you will get more orders.

On being persistent: Did you know 80% of all sales are made after the fifth call? That 48% of salespeople give up after the first call, 25% more give up after the second, 12% more give up after the third call, and 5% more give up after the fourth. Only 10% of all salespeople will make that fifth call, and they will end up with 80% of the sales. Persistence really does pay off.

Body Language

Paying attention to body language, your own and the client's, correlates to the psychology of selling. How much do you squirm around, how much do you click a pen, or are you doing other things that are driving people crazy? I sure have; I've gone through this myself. So be aware of your body language and be aware of your client's body language. For example, are they bored, are they leaning forward, are they sitting back, how interested are they in your product? Make it interesting for them.

Be aware how often you nod your head back and forth, and if you are tapping your legs. Are you moving your arms around? These nervous habits can be very apparent and annoying. Back to clicking a pen—I've seen so many times with other salespeople and myself, we're clicking a pen and not even aware we're doing it. That's why it's important to have friends watch your presentation or have your good clients give you advice, because even if they just say, "Hey, you're clicking a pen and that kind of bugs me," you'll be aware of it and change.

Body language is critical: "open up" rather than having a closed posture! By opening up, you are viewed as more friendly and relaxed.

Don't argue with your client. This is very important in business relationships. There's usually no reason to have an argument with a client. They may get mad, but avoid arguing with them. Let them get upset, and then listen to what they say until they stop talking. Problems will arise: a shipment will be late, something that you've provided doesn't work correctly. There will be problems; some clients will get upset, and even if it's not you personally they're upset with, they may be upset with the factory you represent, or someone else you work with who didn't deliver on time. Just listen and take notes, which shows that you are paying attention and that you intend to work on the situation.

After the client has spoken about their issues, do what is called "reflective listing." Tell the client that you want to repeat back to them so you are sure that you understand exactly what their concerns are. List the topics they mentioned in order, 1, 2, 3, 4, 5, however many there are. After you have done that, find out if there are any other concerns. Simply listen to what they have to say and take notes. Don't make excuses for yourself or the company you represent. The key point is that you allow them to air everything out and that you understand what they have said.

As you listen to what they say, be sure they don't hold back anything. Find out exactly how they feel—it doesn't matter how angry they are. Stay calm and let them know that you are paying attention. Then state what you intend to do about the problem at hand. So again, listen to their concerns without interrupting, and then restate back to them what they said, making sure that you have repeated everything. Then promptly follow up on whatever you said you would do to take care of the problem, and do your best to make the client happy and satisfied.

Releasing a Client

It is okay to fire a client, to get rid of a client. In fact, I encourage you to get rid of some clients. Some sales speakers suggest that at the beginning of every year you should purge ten percent of your clients. I'm not suggesting that you purge ten percent, but if you're not making progress with a client, why keep them? It doesn't make any sense for you or the client. I recommend that you see a client at least five times before you have this conversation. Most of the conversations I've had like this over my career have been with people I've called on for several years and I'm making no money, I'm spinning my wheels, and I don't know the reason why I am not making any sales. Then it's time to have the honest conversation, because I really have nothing to lose.

Contact a client and ask for a time to stop by to have a chat about how you are working together. Let them know that you enjoy calling on them, and that you hope they will use some of your products, even though they haven't to date. Here's the critical thing to say: "I want to know what I can do to work with you in a better way, so that I can get some orders from you," and then be quiet and see what they say. Most people will be honest and tell you why they have not purchased from you if you approach them in a nice way.

In sales, it's inevitable that you will ruffle feathers. You won't get along with everybody, and don't worry about it. But have the honest talk with your client and see what they say. Some people are simply not worth your time. They may not even be aware that they're not buying from you. Or they may be honest with you and they'll say, "I appreciate your coming by, but we've bought from these other two vendors who are your competitors for years. It's good to know about you, but we are probably not going to make any changes." At least you know where you stand with each client, and that is assuring to a salesperson. It's helpful to know if a client is not planning to buy from you. It's fine to quit calling on the client or to send them an email once a year letting them know you are still around, in case they have had any issues with the other vendors they have been buying from. Let them know you are still willing to work with them.

Integrity Comes First

Always be upfront and honest with clients, especially when there is a problem or issue. Acknowledge it if it is your fault. I've been in the floor covering business as a manufacturer's representative for thirty-five years, and shipments get delayed. Sometimes it's the manufacturer's fault, and sometimes the truck driver has a breakdown on the way to the delivery. In any case, be honest. The client may get upset, but they appreciate your telling them the truth. Once you start telling lies, it's a dead-end road. You won't be able to recover from that. The client remembers that you don't always tell them the truth; they will respect you for being honest, even if it's not what they would like to hear. They will respect you, and that's what you're earning—respect.

Anticipate Your Client's Needs

Try to anticipate the client's needs in advance. For example, what do they want to know? Perhaps it's the shipment date, or they need detailed technical information about the product you sell. The point is to get the information to them before they ask for it. When you're working on a project with somebody, provide all the information they need so they can choose what they want, rather than having to call or email you asking for the information. Always be one step ahead of your client by anticipating their needs.

How to do a Better Job

Ask the client how you can do a better job. Your good clients will be honest with you. Tell them you want to do more business with them, and you want to improve your service to them and their company. Let them know that you care about them and that they are very important to you. They will feel very good about you.

Try to have a little humor and laugh at yourself. But be careful with humor because some clients can't handle it. There will always be clients who won't share personal information. They won't talk about themselves or their family, and they don't want to hear any jokes from you. They are 100 percent business. Be aware of this type of client, and be careful with humor.

Consider writing down your notes, rather than typing memos to yourself. You will probably remember something better if you write it rather than type it. Usually people tend to type everything into their phone or their computer. However, the actual writing of the words, as opposed to typing, will help you remember much better.

Good things come out of bad situations. We all will have bad situations in our selling career: something that just doesn't work out right. It's helpful to try to turn negatives into positives. You will lose some orders, of course. If we got every order we worked on, we wouldn't have to work as much as we do. Always work on your batting average, so that your average is higher and each year it keeps getting better. But when you lose an order, call or email your client and let them know that you're sorry you didn't get their order, and that you would like to meet and understand why they didn't purchase your product, or why they purchased from someone else. Go see the client in person and find out what happened. Most salespeople don't do this follow-up.

Usually clients will respect you for this follow-up. Although some people won't give you that time, many will, and then you learn perhaps from a mistake, or why they bought another product. Later you can talk to your manufacturer if you're a manufacturer's rep, or you can talk to your boss or other people in your business. Let them know why you lost this order, and figure out how to avoid that with the next client. Also, when you talk to the client whose order you lost, see how you could work on the next one. There's always a next order—it might be tomorrow, it might be next year. Try to find out what the client's next project will be and mention that you want to start working with them now.

I had a project where there was a little bump in the road, but I was able to turn it into an opportunity to be positive. I had sold a large amount of hard-surface flooring to a hospital over the years, but they were not maintaining it properly. I dealt with several people in my selling cycle: one was an architect, and also the facility managers and maintenance managers at the hospital. The architect called me and said that a little issue had come up at the hospital. The architect was one of the key people, because he had selected the material. Of course, he didn't want to be embarrassed that a product he had selected for his client wasn't performing well. He said that we needed to go look at it. I agreed and was happy to go. But if I had just emailed him the mainte-nance information, it would not have been as effective.

Whatever the situation was, he wanted me to go. I had the opportunity to go to his office, then we rode in his car for fifteen minutes and chatted about several different things, and I got to know him a little better. We went to the job site and dealt with the new person in charge of maintaining the floor. Then we spoke with the project manager at the hospital. We were all there looking at the floor, and I shared the installation and the maintenance information with them. I asked how the floor was being cleaned and with what chemicals. They weren't even sure, which was typical in my industry, because the actual men and women who cleaned the floor weren't there. Their manager, who was new, did not know. But we had a productive meeting. Of course the floor was dirty, but it was a simple matter of not using the right materials to clean the floor. The problem became a win for me because I spent face-to-face time in the car with the architect whom I had known for a long period. He saw that I was there to stand up for him and to take care of the situation. I faced the problems head-on rather than turning away. I planned to go back there in a couple of weeks to meet just with the people who were cleaning the floor to make sure they had the right chemicals. I also contacted the technical person at the manufacturing facility that made this floor. I got him involved on an email, so everybody knew that he was involved.

You are the ringleader as the salesperson. When there are issues, you are the face of the manufacturer or the company you represent. It's up to you to take care of the problem and to get it resolved. In my case, I had time to talk to the architect both driving to the jobsite and driving back. I had the opportunity to speak to him about this project and future projects, and to tell him about other types of flooring products I represented, which he said he was interested in. I sent him an email on these products, and I was able to do more business with him. What could have been a negative situation had a positive outcome. So be aware of these opportunities.

Some clients will get angry with you. Remain calm and do your best to resolve the situation ASAP. Whenever there's a conflict, stay away from the tendency to blame someone. All that does is to escalate the conflict. Try to understand everything that the client has to say about the situation. It's best to meet face to face if you can, and second best is on the phone rather than by email or text. Let the client know that you understand that there's a disagreement or a concern. Ask them to explain it to you, and ask the open-ended question, "Please tell me your concerns about X," and let them talk while you remain quiet.

During the conversation take notes, and, as mentioned earlier, when they're finished explaining all their points repeat back to them each point they have made. Let them totally finish, let them air out their grievances, yell, whatever they need to do. But don't say a word, just take notes. Let them know you want to totally understand their concerns, which is not what most other salespeople tend to do. Consider practicing this technique of listening and repeating back with your sales coach.

When you listen and try to understand, what does that do? It comes down to the other person, because when people really want to be heard, they want you to listen. You don't have to agree with them or say they're right. If you totally think they're wrong, it doesn't matter. The point is that they are being heard by you, and you're taking notes and acknowledging what they are saying. By repeating back to them exactly what they said, you are showing them that you want to understand all their concerns. Then you might say, "I'd like to give you my thoughts on this, I've heard everything that you've said. I have listened carefully, and here's what I'm going to do about it." You're not saying you agree, but you can propose a way to resolve the situation.

You can learn to really enjoy sales psychology. I love getting to know people and learning about people. And I enjoy working on myself so that I can do a better job with each client. As I stated earlier, as salespeople, we are the ones that must change; the client will not change. Working on this will be fun, and it will touch every aspect of your life. And it will lead to profitability for you.

The way we think things are affects us most!
Poor thinking habits keep most people poor.

SmartSelling Strategies: Sales Psychology

- It's important to understand your own psychology and how you behave with other people.
- Be aware of your own strengths and weaknesses.
- In your work as a salesperson, you can't change your clients; you need to adapt to their way of working. Don't expect to change a client.
- Be attentive so you are aware of what type of person your client is: gregarious or more quiet; relaxed or always in a rush.
- Be aware of the tone and the volume of your voice.

- The way you speak with a client will, in part, determine how well they listen to you.
- Find points of common interest to talk about to help build a good business relationship.
- Notice whether or not the person you are talking with is listening to you, or paying attention to their phone or fidgeting.
- Cultivate the art of listening by watching facial expressions and body language.
- Learn to pause during a conversation, and to pause for intervals of a few seconds if you are giving a presentation, so the client has time to think about what you have said.
- Observe yourself as you talk to a client and find out what you need to change.
- Be aware that your clients are always judging you, so observing your own behavior patterns is a way to improve your skill as a salesperson.
- When someone makes a mistake, perhaps misses an appointment, don't take it personally; find out what happened.
- Usually you need to visit a client at least five times in order for them to build their trust in you.
- Try to be friendly and let each client know you have their best interest at heart.
- Avoid arguing with clients about anything.
- When a client is speaking about issues or concerns they have, after they have stated everything, repeat back to them what they have said so they know you listened.
- It's okay to release difficult or unproductive clients.

- It's important to have an honest conversation with a potential client who has never purchased from you—there's no point in wasting their time or yours.
- Always be honest about everything, including problems that come up.
- Anticipate the client's needs in advance, so it's not necessary for them to call you.
- Be aware of opportunities to turn problematic or negative situations into positive outcomes.

I am convinced that life is 10% what happens to me and 90% how I react to it. We are in charge of our own attitudes.

Charles T. Swindoll

It's not the will to win that matters—everyone has that. It's the will to prepare to win that matters.

Paul "Bear" Bryant

4. Follow Up

The Process of Following Up

FOLLOW-UP IS IMPORTANT IN the long-term sales process; there's always something to follow up on with every client and with every project. The salesperson who continually follows up is the one who will do the best and make the most money. Keep close track of the follow-up date for every project, stay organized, and you'll be doing very well. Follow-up is critical and will help you in your sales process.

Follow up on every client and every project until you get your commission check, assuming you are a commissioned salesperson. Keep following up until the order is placed and the product or the service has been delivered. Make sure the client is absolutely satisfied with everything they purchased. Go see the client in person after they have received the product and talk to them about it. Ask how they *feel* about whatever they received from you. The word *feel* evokes more emotion than the word *like*, and the client will probably say more to you. Listen to what they say, and then find out how you can improve anything to make what they bought better for them. Ask an open-ended question so they will give a complete answer, not just yes or no. The very fact that you're asking them about this indicates that you will do your best so they are more satisfied with you and your product or service. If you want to work on the next project with them, a face-to-face visit is very significant.

To be an expert salesperson and to set yourself apart, do the things that other salespeople don't do. Always try to think of the extra little things that you can do; the attention you provide to your client makes you stand out as exceptional. The client will see that you are doing everything possible to help them. Anticipate their needs and their wants regarding the product or service that you sell.

Make the client happy by providing them with information or whatever they need before they call or email you to ask for it. This is a powerful strategy. Think down the road one week, one month, or longer about what the client might need. Each client is different. Maybe one is a very technical person and they want to know all the details about the product or service you're selling them. Send an email stating that you thought they might be interested in more information, and include a link to a website for them to read at their convenience. They will appreciate your being proactive by providing the information they might possibly want.

Always have something to follow up on with each client. This is a long-term sales process, whether you just sold something or you're still working on your first order with them. It might be a five-step process, it might be ten steps. The client is checking you out to see if you actually follow up and if you're organized. There's always something to follow up with each client, so have a date to follow up. That way you always know exactly when to follow up and you know what you will talk about at the next meeting.

The way you ask for the next appointment is very important. While I was still learning the art of being a great salesperson, I would sometimes try to guess when my clients wanted to see me next, and I found that it was not working very well. You must know when a client wants you to talk to them about a specific project. It's usually most effective to be very direct. After you thank the client for meeting with you, ask if there is anything else you can do for them, such as providing additional information on the product or service. Then find out when the appropriate time would be for you to follow up with them again. Put the responsibility on the client to tell you the follow-up date. If they think it will be three or four months before they will be ready, let them know that you will follow up at the time they requested, and put that date in your notes. On the designated date contact them by phone, email, or text. Mention that they suggested that you follow up with them at this time. You're doing what they asked you to do, which is appropriate, and you won't appear to be a pushy salesperson or as being annoying, because you're doing what they asked.

A Follow-up System

Having an efficient follow-up system will set you apart from your competition and you will have a big advantage. Again, most other salespeople will not ask the client when they want them to follow up, they'll just guess at a date to follow up. Sometimes that irritates clients because the salesperson may follow up too soon, or even worse, they'll follow up too late, and then they've missed the sale because they waited too long.

I use a two-tier file system in my office to keep track of projects and their follow-up dates. The top file is for projects that I need to follow up on during the current month, and the bottom file is for any projects requiring follow-up in the next month or later. Don't worry if it's two years from now. A year from now will come, two years from now will come. My follow-up system is on paper. I write down every project, and that's the file for that client. On the top of each page I highlight the key word so the name of the project or client is easy to see. By using a system like this, you have complete information about the client or the project at your fingertips. At the end of each week I take out all information for every project in the top file, which includes projects happening in the current month, and I go through each project. At the end of each month I look at every project in the bottom file. I move any project due for follow-up in the coming month into the top file. That's how I know when to follow up with each client.

Design your follow-up system in any way that works for you. When I work with you one-on-one, or in a group with your company, I will not try to convince you to use my system. We're all different, and you need to feel comfortable with your system, which I can help you design. As long as you have a follow-up date with every project and every client, you will be organized with your follow-up. It doesn't matter whether the date is next week or next year. You know what you need to do next with each client, and it's helpful to be able to quickly find the project or the client and the basic information that you require.

Responding to Clients

Check messages as soon as possible and get back to people promptly. If you're the one who immediately gets back to your clients when they text, email, or phone you, you will be way ahead of your competition. Clients want answers now! So the quicker you can get back to your client, the more professional you will come across to them; remember, your clients are constantly judging you. If someone calls you unexpectedly and you reply to them promptly, it's very significant because they're probably not calling just to say hi. They may need to solve a problem, which is part of your job as a sales professional: solving problems for people. When you're solving an issue for someone, the quicker you can get back to them, the better it is for both of you.

Leave time between sales calls to check your messages and attend to other tasks that come up. If you have five outside sales calls, don't cram them too close to each other, so you're rushing from one appointment to the next. Space out the appointments. It may be efficient to allow an hour for a half-hour appointment. It's not professional to say, "I've got to go to my next appointment." Leave yourself time for driving and time to sit in the car to make notes on the meeting you just had. Review the notes you've already taken, and think about the meeting and add additional details that you might not have had time to write down. It's essential to remember everything your client tells you for future follow-up.

Between appointments is also a convenient time to check voice messages, texts, and emails. It's ideal to respond immediately to the most important messages. Don't ignore your messages for an entire day. You will be overwhelmed at the office when you're trying to get back to these people. If you don't reply to them until 4:30 or 5:00, they may not see the message until the next day. Be proactive and reply as quickly as possible. So again, make time in between sales calls to take a few deep breaths, relax, and check your messages, and get back to these clients right away.

Never give up!

In the follow-up system, the details are very important. It's the little things that you either do right or don't do right that every client notices. So take the time to follow up properly on every project and every client, and that means having good, detailed notes, so that one week or one year from now, you can refer to your notes and know exactly what you meant and what the client expects.

For outstanding success, become really great at follow-up; it's absolutely the key. You are in a long-term business relationship with a client, and following up at the right time and working the way the client wants you to work are what's important, not the way you want to work. You need to adjust to the client and follow up when they want you to follow up.

SmartSelling Strategies: Follow Up

- The salesperson who continually follows up is the one who will do the best and make the most money.
- Leave time between sales calls to check your messages and attend to other tasks that come up.
- After delivery, contact your client and ask how they feel about the product or service they have received from you.
- Anticipate the client's needs and wants regarding the product or service that you sell.
- Find out when the appropriate time would be for you to follow up next with a client, then meet at the time they request.
- When you're organized, whenever a client calls or emails you looking for information about their purchase, you can quickly find it for them.
- Take time in between sales calls to take a few deep breaths and relax, and then check your messages and get back to the clients right away.
- Clients will need your help in solving problems; this is part of your job as a sales professional.
- It's the little things that you either do right or don't do right that every client notices.

*For every sale you miss because
you're too enthusiastic, you will
miss a hundred because you're not
enthusiastic enough.*
Zig Ziglar

*Continuous effort—not strength
or intelligence—is the key to
unlocking your potential.*
Liane Cardes

5. Listening and Communication

YOUR SKILLS IN LISTENING and communication are crucial to your success in sales. Using these skills wisely is very strategic with your clients. Taking notes shows your client that you are listening and it reinforces that you care about what they are saying. Also, taking notes helps you remember the conversation. For additional discussion on the art of listening, refer to chapter three, Sales Psychology.

One of the most important aspects of listening is to listen without the intent to respond. Most people listen to respond, and in our society we constantly interrupt each other, whether we are at a family get-together or in a business meeting. If you can truly listen to what the client is saying and take notes, you will be way ahead of many salespeople. Remember to pause during the conversation to allow your client time to think about what they want to say.

It's beneficial for you not to interrupt during a conversation. When you interrupt your client, they will probably stop talking, and that's not helpful to you. When the client has a lot to say, you get to know the client. And the more they talk, they will feel more comfortable with you and they will continue to open up to you.

Great listeners are usually well-liked people. This has been confirmed in psychology over and over. When you are getting to know someone, encourage them to talk about their work and their life. If you can motivate the other person to talk by asking open-ended questions, when they leave they will say, "Wow, that person is really a fun person to get to know." What they don't consciously realize is that they did ninety percent of the talking. But because you have the skill of being an attentive listener and keeping quiet, you are perceived as being very likeable. The more they talk about something personal, the more they will like you. It's fantastic in a relationship and it's so easy for salespeople to use our ears more and our mouth less.

Words that will make people like you:
Thank you!; You're welcome; Here's what's happening; How can I help?; I'll find out; I believe in you.

While you are listening, taking notes shows the client that you are truly interested—that you care about them. Hopefully you will be business friends for years with these people. Not every client will turn out that way, but it's a useful goal when starting out with a client. In two months, two years, or twenty years out, you will be able to refer back to your notes covering whatever you have talked to this person about. Also, taking notes keeps you from speaking. Just stay calm, listen, and take notes. The client will feel happy that you're taking notes about them. It's fun for you, and you're getting to know the client when they talk about their family or vacations they've been on, their pets, or anything else personal.

Here's another key point for effective communication. When the client is about to stop talking, don't look them in the eye. When a person starts to slow down or stops speaking, they're not quite sure what they want to say next. If you interrupt or stare at them, they will shut down. Give the client as much as five seconds—that's hard to do. Give them time to get their thoughts together about what they want to say next.

An interesting fact regarding communication is that about fifty-five percent of what another person "hears" from what you are saying is nonverbal. That's very significant. For example, they note how fast you are talking. I am constantly working on these habits: how loud I am speaking; the tone of my voice; whether I am smiling or not smiling. People are aware of all these things.

When you are talking to your clients, while fifty-five percent of the communication is nonverbal, thirty-eight percent is the tone of your voice. We all have experienced this in various aspects of our lives. Someone has probably told you, "Hey, I don't like the tone of your voice!" Or you're aware of another person's tone of voice; this is a huge part of communication. Only seven percent of what the client hears is the actual words you say.

Pay attention to your own body movements. Are you constantly clicking a pen? Are you doing things that drive people nuts? I have, I've tapped my foot, I've done all kinds of things I wasn't aware of. Become aware of your annoying nervous habits. The client will pick up on all those behaviors.

It can be helpful to look in the mirror when you are practicing for an important talk. Also, get feedback from your friends and associates on the way you communicate, because they'll be honest and they want you to succeed in your sales career. You might also get good ideas from your best clients. Just ask for their feedback.

In any conversation, allow the client to speak more than you do. When a client is talking more than you are, it shows that they want to do business with you because they're giving you information. If they're not interested in you or they don't like you, or they're not interested in your product, they will just stop talking and sit there quietly, hoping that you will leave soon. Pay attention to the client's body language and act accordingly.

As a good listener, remember that you have two ears and one mouth. If you think about using your ears twice as much as your mouth, you'll be doing very well. It's essential to realize that as a salesperson, it's not about us, it's about the client. So avoid doing what I call "one up" the person. When a client starts talking about a vacation they've been on, or where they've lived in any part of the world, the last thing you want to do is to say, "Oh I've lived there, too," or "I've traveled to Europe also." They don't care at that point, but down the road they will. But especially when you are getting to know them, it's not about you at all, it's about them! You will have the chance to tell your story later. Many salespeople think they must tell everything about their product or about themselves right at the beginning, but it's not necessary. Wait until later to tell the client about things you have in common. You'll have plenty of opportunity to do that.

When you're talking with a client and want to get more information from them, ask open-ended questions rather than closed-ended questions. Closed-ended questions require only a one- or two-word answer: Will you please tell me your name? They will state their name and then stop talking. Do you like the color green? That's a closed-ended question. The following are examples of open-ended inquiries: Tell me how long you've been at this company; Tell me about your family; Tell me about this beautiful picture on your wall. You will learn a lot. Especially during the first several times you meet with a new client and are getting to know them, asking open-ended questions will encourage them to speak. Also, when a client talks more with open-ended questions, they feel more comfortable. They're not pinned down, and they can tell you as much or as little as they want to.

My daughter is twenty-five now, but when she was little she would come home with a drawing and I did not know what she had drawn. Now she's a pretty good artist, but I would say to her, "What is that?" That didn't go over very well, and she would get upset. My wife has taught me many things over the years, and she taught me the words, "Tell me" because when I would say, "Tell me about that drawing," my daughter could say whatever she wanted. In the same way, when you say the words "Tell me" to your client, it gives them the opportunity to open up and share whatever they want to tell you.

Work on asking engaging, open-ended questions; it does take skill and it takes time. Write down starter lines such as, "Tell me . . ." or "Please tell me . . ." or "I'm curious to know . . .," anything that you feel comfortable with, and then start incorporating this information into your conversations. Doing this with your friends also will help you in all aspects of your life. The person you're listening to will feel important. Listening and developing great communication skills will be fun for you and lead to great profits.

SmartSelling Strategies: Listening and Communication

- "First seek to understand, then seek to be understood." (Stephen Covey)
- Your skills in listening and communication will help you be a successful salesperson.
- Take good notes when you are working with clients; it shows your clients you are listening and it reinforces your communication.
- While you are listening, taking notes shows the client that you're really interested in them.
- When the client is about to stop talking, don't look them in the eye; allow them time to figure out what to say next.
- It's important to realize that as a salesperson it's not about us, it's about the client.
- Among listening and communication skills, one of the most important is to listen without the intent to respond.

I never left the field saying I could have done more to get ready, and that gives me peace of mind.

Peyton Manning

Customers are the most important people in every business! Customers do not depend on us, we depend on them.

LL Bean Company

6. Prospecting: Finding Your Clients

Growing Your Client Base

SALES IS A NUMBERS game: see more people, track more projects, and make more money. Part of being organized in sales is having a system to build a strong client and project portfolio. To be an effective and successful salesperson, an ongoing process in your planning and organization is finding your clients and expanding your database, whether you are a new salesperson or are experienced in your industry. You can't go anywhere without a client. You need a client to make a sale. Ten clients who are good clients, clients you take care of all the time, will be more productive for you than twice as many clients who don't receive your full attention.

Think about the quality of each sales call versus the number of sales calls that you make.

Be on the outlook for new clients; you never know when you will find those. You might meet them in a social function or through friends and family, but always have your ears open and be aware that somebody might be talking about something that could help you in your business. Constantly being aware of information floating around can be helpful in finding new clients. Always do a very professional job, and also continually add to the number of clients you serve. At the same time, clients who are well taken care of by you will be loyal.

Cold Calling

Cold calling to find new clients is a fun part of the sales process. I've been in sales for thirty-five years, and I enjoy walking into a building when the only purpose is to meet people. With practice, you will become comfortable with the simple process of cold calling. Many people in sales fear cold calling, but it's actually entertaining if you know what to do and you use a friendly approach, such as the one explained here.

Meeting the Receptionist

Think of cold calling as meeting new friends. That's really all you're doing. When you walk through the front door you have two main objectives. One is to meet the receptionist very briefly and get to know him or her. Don't try to talk right away about the product or service you sell. When you walk up to the receptionist, mention anything other than what you're selling—just be friendly, and find out their name. The second thing to do is to find out the name of the person who is the decision maker for whatever product or service you're selling, and then leave. Those are really the only two things to do. It's not necessary to take a lot of information with you on a cold call. It's an introductory meeting; think of a cold call as the first step in the long sales process. Cold calling is a very important part of the sales process, and should be incorporated into your daily and weekly routine between other sales calls or when you just want to spend a few hours here and there making cold calls.

After the cold call, write down the receptionist's name and write down the name of the decision maker for the product or service you sell. You can talk about the weather, talk about a picture on their wall, or you could say, "Wow, this is really a pretty office. Tell me about this office." Say anything to get them to talk a little bit. They know you're a salesperson—that will be obvious to them, it won't be a secret. They deal with this every day, but if you do something to establish a rapport, it's easier for both of you. Help the receptionist to feel comfortable with you. Because this is a long-term sales process, you will know this receptionist over a long period, as you're selling to this company.

Remember, you're meeting the receptionist and trying to find out who the decision maker is, and you want the receptionist to talk. It's similar to any time you're in front of a client; the more you can get them to speak and you are quiet, the better you'll do. Write down whatever they say that might be of interest, whether it's about their family or about the building they work in or how long they have worked at that particular company. Find a topic that you can use to connect with that person, so the next time you see him or her when you walk in, you have something to talk about as an icebreaker.

Make your confidence high
and your stress low!

It's important to be focused and really listen. Listening and hearing are two totally different processes. We hear all the time, but rarely do we listen; listen very carefully to what the receptionist says and make notes. If the receptionist is busy on the phone or someone is at their desk, stand back, away from them. Don't crowd the receptionist, because that will make them feel uncomfortable. You would feel the same way if you were the receptionist and someone was hovering over you. Give some space and wait until the receptionist is ready to talk to you.

Stay Focused

While you are waiting in a lobby, don't be busy with your phone or tablet, don't do other business tasks while you're waiting for the receptionist to acknowledge you. Be aware of the people who are walking through the office. You never know when the owner of the company or the decision maker might walk by. Just a simple "hello" and a smile are wonderful to do when someone walks by; you may not know who they are, but they will remember you. If the next week or two weeks later you happen to be calling on that firm again, they could be the person you want to see.

Watch, listen, and learn while you're waiting for the receptionist. Learn as much as you can about the company.

You never know what you'll see on the wall: pictures of the founder of the company, pictures concerning the history of the company, so be observant while you're waiting for the receptionist to call you. I've met many interesting people while waiting in a lobby. Sometimes it's the person that you need to see later, so be a friendly face. Again, don't be looking at your phone or iPad; you are there to get to know the people at that business.

Plan to stay only one or two minutes once you approach the receptionist, because they are busy. The last thing to do is to linger and create a problem on the first sales call. No matter how friendly the receptionist is, even if there's nobody in the lobby or the receptionist doesn't look busy, make a point to only stay a couple of minutes.

Because the goal is to get the contact information of the decision maker, it is important to give your card to the receptionist for them to give to the decision maker. Remember to say "please" when you ask them to pass on the card. And if you give two cards to the receptionist, they can keep one and have something to remember you by. You now have a business relationship when you call that office. Anytime you go in, say hi to the receptionist.

When you give the receptionist a card to pass on to the decision maker, remember to use the words "please" and "thank you." In my opinion, these meaningful words are underused in the sales profession. If you say, "Please, I'd really appreciate your giving this card to the decision maker" (mention the name of the person that he or she told you is the decision maker), and you let them know that you will follow up soon with that individual, they will most likely give the card to the person who makes the decisions.

Then actually do the follow-up. Refer to chapter four, Follow Up, for more information on the process of following up. You will always be following up on something, so follow up a couple of days after your first visit with an email to the receptionist. Think about this: how many people in sales take the time to send a thank-you note to the receptionist? Aim to set yourself apart from your competitors. The little things you do become the big things in any aspect of life and in sales, too. Becoming a friend with the receptionist will go a long way, because the receptionist knows everything that's going on in that office.

Have a purpose in what you do.

Send an email thanking the receptionist, and remember to use their name when you meet again. People love to hear their name; it's meaningful to them. As you know, if you're in a crowd somewhere and somebody says your name, you'll hear it even if you're talking to someone else. The receptionist will appreciate hearing his or her name; it's another one of those little gestures that makes a big difference.

Calling the Decision Maker

Call the decision maker a few days after you've sent the thank-you note or email to the receptionist. When you call the decision maker, if the receptionist answers they will remember you. When you first contact the decision maker, calling is preferable, rather than sending an email. Most likely you will get the receptionist on the phone, and because they know who you are, say hi and that you enjoyed visiting with them, and ask if they could please connect you with the decision maker. When you speak to the decision-making person on the phone the first time, mention the receptionist's name. Then that person is aware that you know who the receptionist is, and they're much more likely to be pleasant to you because you've taken the time to meet the receptionist.

Next, inform the decision maker about the product or service you represent, and tell them that you would like to stop by their office for a minute or two just to say hi. That is so strategic, because most salespeople take advantage of these situations and will spend thirty minutes or an hour on a first sales call, and the client won't like that. They're much more likely to meet with you if you let them know it will be a very short visit. Assume that you're the buyer of a product or service and you deal with salespeople all the time, and you've got many things going on. If a salesperson says they would like to come by for one or two minutes just to say hi, the odds are good that you would do that.

Look at the first sales call to the decision maker as simply getting to know them. It's very important to keep the first visit brief. You don't even need to sit down, just go by and say, "Thank you for giving me a few minutes of your time." Shake hands and tell them a little bit about yourself, and they may ask you to come in to their office to chat. That's fine if they do, but if they don't, just spend one or two minutes with them and leave, because you'll have something to follow up on the next time.

Remember that it's helpful when the receptionist is your friend, because they are a critical person to you when you are looking for new clients; most salespeople overlook this. If you're the person who is friendly with the receptionist, they will be helpful to you. The receptionist can help you in whatever you're selling, because they know everything that's going on there. In short, cold calls can be fun, and you have nothing to lose with a cold call when you go in to meet the receptionist.

I suggest that you first schedule cold calls for an area familiar to you, and walk into familiar buildings to practice becoming good at cold calls. Make cold calls between other calls. There will be many occasions in your sales career when you will have time in between set appointments to stop in a couple of office buildings to meet the receptionist. It takes practice to do this right, but there is no need to fear it. Start making cold calls now. I know that I have made a lot of money by making cold calls over my many years of selling.

Adding New Projects and Clients

Your success will grow as you constantly add new projects and new prospects to your list. Along the way you will lose some clients. So it's essential to always be adding more clients. Cold calling is one important way to find new prospects. Also, talk to friends and associates and let people know what you do and try to get more projects in the pipeline. Or you can start a business relationship with an individual or a company and tell them what you do, and then always have a follow-up time. There's always something that you can follow up on with each of those prospects.

It is very important to be constantly adding new people to your list because sales comes down to a numbers game; you can't make a living unless you have enough clients to bring you the yearly income you need. Most likely, depending on what you sell, you will need several hundred clients. Think about ways to meet new people and add them to your list. Think about people you know and who knows you. These are different: you may know a hundred people but only ten people know who you are and what you do. It is helpful for people to know you and know what you do; they may send referrals to you or send you to a new prospect.

You will be on the way to success if you know a hundred people and ninety or a hundred of them know exactly what you do. Take the time to educate your friends and others in your life about what you do, so they can help you in your sales career. Stay in touch with everyone, because you never know who that next client will be. Just staying in touch with people is important. I've had many clients and many big projects that I've earned by staying in contact with someone for many years. I sometimes tell my wife that I just got a big order from a particular client, and she reminds me that I've been working with this client for many years. She is, of course, exactly right. By staying in touch with these people and letting them know in a friendly way what you do, whether by email, a newsletter, or social media, these people constantly know what you do. You never know when the next opportunity will come about. I had one project that is a good example of a successful outcome in a long-standing relationship.

I live in Albuquerque, New Mexico, and I work with a number of architects. This architect I had known for approximately twenty years, and I made a little money working with him on some very small projects. Then suddenly he called me and he had a big project with one of his private clients. He said, "Look, Eddy, I want you to take care of this. This client knows what he wants, he wants it done, and he wants it done right." I jumped on it right away, I met with this architect and his client, and I took care of it and everybody was happy. And I was happy because I made good money on the project. It was because of my relationship with that architect, and his client trusted him when I was brought in as the flooring expert. Be the expert in your field and always have new information and knowledge to pass along to your customers.

When you are working on finding new clients, friends and family are the easiest to start with as possible resources. If you're a new salesperson, or if you're an experienced salesperson but starting with a new line or with a new company, or maybe you're in a different industry than you've been in before, talk to your friends, talk to your family, and have meetings with them. When you meet for coffee let them know you have started a new career or that you are new in sales, or you are in a new industry. Tell them what you are selling, and that you want them to know about it.

This approach of talking with friends and family serves a couple of purposes. You can practice your casual presentation, because your friends and family will be nice to you. There will be some people who won't be so nice to you if you falter on your presentation or you forget something. But your friends will be supportive and understanding, or if they give you a bit of hard time, it will be in good fun. I'm constantly surprised; I'll take a group of friends and associates, people who work at the same office, out to lunch, for example, and we'll talk about anything other than what I'm selling. We'll talk about a city that somebody has been to or used to live in, and it always happens that one of the other people has been there, or used to live there, too. They'll find out something about each other. I'm amazed that these people work at the next desk or in the same office building, on the same floor, and they know nothing about each other. So friends and family are a perfect place to start and get the word out because they can help you by being a good audience. And they might have leads for you, they might have ideas, and they might refer people to you or suggest that you contact a particular person.

It's beneficial for your business to join as many groups as you can and to do volunteer work as well. Join business groups, networking groups, and volunteer and service groups. I wish I could have done volunteer work my whole sales career, but there have been times when I just haven't been able to. Now, fortunately, I'm in a position where I can do quite a bit of volunteer work, which I really enjoy. It's fun to get into conversations with people. We're all volunteers spending time at the same place, and everyone wants to know what you do. When you help other people by doing volunteer work, it comes back to help you.

When you get together in groups and exchange information about what's going on, those involvements are all helpful. Don't overwhelm yourself and don't try to get in more groups than you can handle. Start with one and see how it goes; if you want to add more groups, do so when you are ready.

Marketing and Promotion Using Social Media

If you are an employee of a company, the primary marketing of your products will probably be handled by the company. However, if you are an independent salesperson and the responsibility for marketing is yours, or if you are new at sales, you may want to consider taking a short course in basic marketing. There are many courses offered online designed to be completed at your own pace and in your own time. Also, explore new marketing strategies that will help you advance your market outreach. It's essential to know how to use social media connections and new technology options. Social media is here, and can be very effective if you are willing to give it a try. Not only is social media a vital way to connect in the business world, but it's the way to keep up with what's going on in your clients' lives and with other people you will be calling on. If you post a comment on a client's page, they will be pleased that you took time and noticed them with a short reply. I don't view social media as a substitute for personal calls, but it may be the way that many clients prefer to get current information.

There are many good social media experts to help steer you or your company in the right direction. A blog is one way to go, and there are many free blog services. Or consider building a Facebook page. Facebook is a simple and timely way to update clients on new products, technology, and promotions you may be offering. It's easy to post photos on your Facebook timeline. Also, consider putting links to Facebook, Flickr, Twitter, LinkedIn and/or Pinterest on your website to provide current information on you and your company. LinkedIn is targeted for business connections more than the others. In any case, be aware of the group etiquette for each of the social media and how social media can benefit you.

An opportunity to extend your exposure from social media is to link back to your own website from your social media pages. Paid advertising and targeted promotions are other possibilities in social media. But it does take time to accumulate a long list of friends, "likes" and "tweets." When you add new names to your email contacts and database, be sure to add those to your social media for the widest exposure. At the same time, keep your social media pages current and updated, especially your profiles. Set aside time in your schedule to post on your pages at least once during the week. A "dead" page won't attract a new client.

While many business people think social media is far more efficient than attending trade shows and making face-to-face calls for establishing contacts, there are others who believe that social media is a waste of time in terms of business return. You won't know for yourself and your business unless you give it a try. Become familiar with social media and learn how the various platforms might work for you and how people communicate using them. At the same time, social media doesn't necessarily mark the end of person-to-person, across-the-desk relationships. The two approaches can work together for you.

It's essential these days to have your own engaging website. Even one page will do. Your website projects the image you want to present for yourself and your products. The site doesn't need to be entirely promotional. A little humor may engage your audience. Be sure the site is professionally designed and written, and that it offers easy access or links for people to contact you directly from your site. Strike a balance between business updates and a bit of personal news that is related to your business, perhaps some news about an upcoming trip or a new book that you found to be very helpful. Your website should also accurately reflect the information that you present in your social media pages. You might want to include FAQs about your products and services and a contact form for prospective clients to request specific information about you, your services, and your products. Your web page is also an opportunity to post pictures of completed projects that have some unique appeal to show off your talents. It's also appropriate to include testimonials from satisfied clients on your page.

Whether you are reaching out by phone, email, social media, or in person, all inquiries from prospective clients deserve timely responses. Personally-tailored responses will be the most helpful in developing a relationship. If you find you don't have enough time in your schedule to follow through with emails and online marketing, you may want to consider hiring a part-time assistant or a marketing consultant to do this for you, particularly if your web presence is helping to build your business. It may be practical to train your assistant with information about your products and let them do the posting, and save yourself some time.

SmartSelling Strategies — Prospecting: Finding Your Clients

- Sales is a numbers game: see more people, track more projects, and make more money.
- Have only as many clients as you can comfortably manage.
- The only purpose of a cold call is to meet people, it is not to sell anything.
- Think of cold calling as meeting new friends.
- The goal of cold calling is to meet the receptionist and to find out who the decision maker is for purchasing products that you sell.
- Talk to family, friends, and associates to find new clients.
- It's important for people you know to know what you do, so they can refer others to you.
- Be alert; you never know where the next client is coming from.
- Joining groups and doing volunteer work are great ways to find new clients.
- The quality of every client meeting you have is more important than the number of meetings you have.
- You will benefit by developing the skill of listening and taking notes as you listen.
- When you are waiting in the lobby to meet the receptionist, stay focused on what is going on around you; you might meet the next important person you need to know.
- Keep your first visit with the receptionist very brief, just a couple of minutes.

- Always remember to call the receptionist by their name; it will help them connect with you.
- When you speak with the decision maker for the first time, remember to mention the receptionist's name.
- Keep your social media and online presence current so your clients have the latest information you want to share.

An effective follow-up system is the key to an effective coaching process, which will lead to significant behavioral changes. True success is in the follow-up.

Farshad Asi

Every great athlete, artist, and aspiring being has a great team to help them flourish and succeed—personally and professionally. Even the so-called 'solo star' has a strong supporting cast helping them shine, thrive and take flight.

Rasheed Ogunlaru

7. Sales Techniques

Meeting the Decision Maker

THE FIRST STEP IN developing and using good sales techniques is to fine-tune your skills for meeting people, and to know how to find out who the decision maker is for your product or your service in a particular company. Many salespeople fall into a trap of not getting to the person they really need to meet in order to sell their product or services. For example, you might meet the receptionist, and the receptionist will suggest that you talk to someone else, and then you talk to that person, but they really don't make the decision or have any influence. It's very important to find out who the actual decision maker is and to meet that individual. If the decision maker does not meet with you, maybe their assistant will. Most likely, the assistant will pass on the information to the proper person.

You might have to work your way up the ladder and talk to the assistant first, before you have the opportunity to speak with the decision maker. The decision maker may not meet with you initially because they don't know you, and they want to see how you will do talking with the assistant. The decision maker may want to see what the assistant has to say about you, so the assistant, of course, will report to the decision maker. When you're finished speaking with the assistant, it's important to thank them for their time because they are a significant person in the sales process. Mention that you look forward to their passing on the information to the person they work with. But the key outcome is that you know who the decision maker is, so that at some point you get to know that person as well.

When you are seated in a meeting about your products and services, it's appropriate to ask the person who shows up who the decision maker actually is. Or if you go to see someone specific and a different person meets you, ask them about the decision maker. Introduce yourself and tell them what your product or service is. Find out what their position is at the company, and if they are the one who makes the decisions on the products or services you sell. They will usually tell you. They may be an intern or they may be new, and their assignment is to meet with sales representatives. Their job may be to get the information from you and pass that along to their boss.

This is not an uncommon situation, so be very professional with the person who meets you, and assume that this person will influence or determine the decision, and that you may or may not get the opportunity to talk to the boss. The reality is that if you don't do a good job talking to this person, you'll never have the opportunity to talk to somebody else.

Meeting the Decision Maker's Staff

I came up with a strategy several years ago for meeting the actual decision maker. You may occasionally have trouble getting an appointment and meeting with the decision maker or meeting with anyone involved with purchasing at a firm. Here's an approach to consider if you are not able to connect with the president of the company or the buyer, or whoever makes the decision regarding your products and services. Call the receptionist and find out who the secretary or assistant is for the person making purchase decisions. Ask for their name. As mentioned earlier, if you already have a good, friendly relationship with the receptionist, this should be very easy.

When you call, mention to the receptionist that they told you to meet with a particular decision-making person, and explain that it has been difficult because he or she doesn't respond to your emails or phone calls. Ask the receptionist to please give you the name of that person's assistant, and they will probably do that. Then call the assistant. Introduce yourself and say that you would like to come by and say hi for a couple minutes and give them a little information about your product. Most likely the assistant will be taken off-guard, because who has ever called to meet with him or her? They are the assistant to the boss, and they will be flattered.

It has been my experience that if you ask to see the assistant for a couple of minutes, they will probably agree. Mention that you have been trying to get in touch with their supervisor or boss, and you want them to know about your product or service. This will be effective because the assistant will pass it along to their superior, and your product will be seen and heard about by the actual decision maker. Also, the assistant or the secretary, like the receptionist, knows what is going on with the company. Sometimes it seems that they know more than the boss, because the boss relies on the assistant for many things. So the assistants are very powerful people for you to become friends with, just as the receptionists are.

Cold Calling Techniques

Another aspect of sales techniques is building your skills to do a lot of cold calling. Every person you talk to at any company is important, whether it's the receptionist or the person who sweeps the floors, so speak professionally to everyone. I have a class in my webinar series about cold calls, and cold calls are discussed in chapter six about prospecting. Your only mission for a cold call is to walk in the door, smile, and get to know the receptionist. Make sure you know his or her name, then find out the name of the person you should talk to about your products and services.

It is a very effective sales technique to know the receptionist's name. The receptionist is critical to you, so keep a note of their name and always refer to them by name. It's important to become good at memorizing names. If you need to have a name list at your fingertips, that's fine; keep it in your car on a piece of paper or notepad. Right before you walk in, memorize the names of the receptionist and other people you may have met or will be meeting at that company.

Again, the receptionist is an important person for you because they know most everything going on in that office. Most salespeople don't get to know the receptionist; I do, and it has helped me a lot. Get to know the receptionist and everybody at that office because you never know who can be influential in the sales process, so that you can get your products or your services sold to that company.

Working Hours

People need to have free time, and as salespeople we need to be organized and work smart.

The number of hours you work each week is not as important as the quality of your work and how smart you work. Some people like to brag about how many hours they work each day or each week, and they think that's impressive. But we all need to have free time, and we need to be organized and work smart. Always think about working smart, not the number of hours you work each week. It's a very important aspect of sales techniques to be well organized so you can maybe work fewer hours than you did the year before and still make the same amount of money, or make even more money because you're more efficient in each day.

Being efficient is key to being successful in sales. Again, the number of sales calls you make each day is not as important as the quality of the calls. I've had clients who are sales managers, and they tell me how important it is for their salespeople to make a specific number of sales calls each day. Salespeople, like anybody else, want to do what we're supposed to do. But if we don't make a specific number of calls that day, what are we going to do? Instead of fabricating a story about the calls you made, I encourage you to think about the quality of each sales call versus the number of sales calls that you make.

Presenting Your Products and Services

> A presentation without a demonstration
> is just a conversation.

Your presentation of the features and benefits of your products will be more interesting when you do a demonstration. Everyone may not remember your name, but they will remember the demonstration you do. I'm an amateur juggler, so sometimes I juggle during a presentation. The clients remember me because I juggle, and it also keeps them awake. If you do a demonstration that relates to a benefit of the product or service you are selling, clients will remember that. Six months later, they'll recall, "Oh yeah, that person did a demonstration on . . .," and they'll remember that the demonstration correlated to the product or service you sell. If they were not the only one in the office who was listening to your presentation, they may say to somebody else, "Who was that person who did that demonstration about . . .?" Demonstrations have an impact and make you memorable to your clients, especially when you allow the client to get involved in the demonstration.

Do not attempt to show everything to a client on the first sales call. This is a very helpful sales technique. Salespeople often bring in way too much for the buyer or the purchasing manager, and it only overwhelms them. Plan to be brief in the first meeting. Don't bring in ten catalogs to somebody the first time you see them; it's too much. Bring in one or two, and then have a follow-up date and a follow-up plan. Remember—look at sales as a long-term process of building a good business relationship. If you have ten points that you want to get across to someone, and you know that buying this particular product or service takes a certain period of time, you can present the information in blocks of twenty percent. If you have ten items to show someone, each time take in two to show the person. After five visits you've shown everything that you want to present. If you have a hundred items, present them in increments. You will see this person a minimum of five times. Each time show them a few products, make your point, and then quickly review the information the next time you're with them. Mention that you spoke about this at the previous meeting, and talk about it for thirty seconds. Then show them a different feature of the product, and always explain the benefit to them. It's what's in it for them, not just the feature—but what the benefit is for them. When you present the information about features and benefits in small increments, you have the opportunity to see the client over and over, which is strategic because repeat visits are the best way to build your business relationship with them.

Always have a next step with each client. Often salespeople think they don't need to know much about sales techniques. They go in and show everything they have. That's not really the way sales works, unless maybe you're selling low-ticket items like pencils or pens or other inexpensive items. But if you're selling products that cost a thousand dollars or more, you need to have a system and you need to always know what the next step is in the process with each client. The process will be different with each situation.

Decision-making Time

It is important to be face to face with the client when they're ready to decide on a purchase. Use your psychology skills and ask your client at the appropriate time when they think they will be ready to decide on the product. You know they're talking to your competitors. But let them know that you would like to review everything that you've talked about very briefly. Be there face to face at the time when they will be making a decision and find out if they have any questions. Ask them how they think your product or service compares to your competitors' products. If you are the only one who shows up that week and they haven't talked to your competitors for two or three months, they may rely on you more. They will probably let you know what they like about a particular product from someone else who is selling the same type of product. Or they may be attracted to some service the person offers. You can acknowledge that they have an interesting point and that you realize it is an advantage of that product or service. But an important technique is to tell them about a very similar feature of your product; explain it or demonstrate it, and be there when he or she is making the decision.

Be a Problem Solver, Sell Solutions

Be a source of solutions to your client's problems. They all know that you're there to sell something, but if you help to solve a problem, you become very popular. You have freed up some time for the busy person who is buying the product or service from you. If you can assist them by quickly getting the information they need, it will help build a long-term business relationship. Don't be just another salesperson. Eighty percent of your competitors are just "ordinary" salespeople. They probably don't understand how to build a business relationship, and they don't practice these sales techniques.

By working with me as a consultant and by utilizing the strategies and techniques presented here, you are setting yourself apart from eighty to ninety percent of your competitors. So follow this advice, and tweak it to make it work for you. Limit your competition and make yourself much more important to the person you're working with, your client. Clients want to work with people who make their problems go away. Perhaps someone in the company holds a particular position because they are capable of dealing with issues, and if you can help them, they will appreciate you. When they have items to purchase, such as the types of products or services you sell, they will remember you.

If you occasionally spend a few minutes with them and take care of their needs in the category of product or service you sell, you will be appreciated. Sell solutions; keep in mind that you are selling solutions to problems and you are not simply a salesperson. People buy products to solve their problems. When you make a purchase, you often want a specific type of product to solve a particular problem; that's what your clients want also.

Earning New Business

Ask new clients how you can earn their business. The word *earn* is very powerful, because you have to work hard to earn the business of new clients. But remember, even when you are thinking of new clients, you need to continue to work with ongoing clients as well.

Whether you are thinking of new clients or ongoing clients, always think about how you can do a better job. This is about earning the respect and trust of those new clients. Let them know that you want to earn their trust, because every client is different. We are not mind-readers of the new clients. The client may think we know everything they are thinking, but we really don't. Ask them how you can earn their business, and tell them that you want to work hard to earn their business and get some orders with them. Clients will appreciate that you are saying this, because most salespeople don't. When you ask a potential new client, "How can I earn your business?" what does that do for you? That's an open-ended question, not a yes or no, so they will most likely tell you, and they may talk for two or three minutes. They may tell you how bad the competitors are or how great the competitors are. Find out about how they've been buying this type of product or service in the past. They will offer a lot of information when you ask the question, "How I can earn your business?" Telling clients that you want to work hard for them and you want to earn each order is also important, because it separates you from just being a salesperson coming in and showing your product, and hoping that they buy something. You're trying to solve their problems and build a long-term business relationship with them.

The First Sales Call—Keep it Brief

Make the first sales call very brief. Using this sales technique will win you new clients. Many salespeople waste the client's time, especially on the first sales call. Tell the person via email or phone that you want to come in to meet for ten to fifteen minutes, and stick to that. The client wants the first meeting to be brief, so you're on the same page with them. Most people don't want to spend half an hour or an hour with a salesperson on the first sales call. All they're trying to do is get to know you and you are wanting to get to know them.

Tell them a few words about yourself, find out a little about them, give them a little information about your product, and leave. Leaving after a few minutes is very important: kick yourself out after letting them know that you appreciate the ten minutes they spent with you. You might say: "I'm going to be on my way now because I know you have other things to do. When would be the appropriate time to follow up with you?" Then set the next meeting, because that's what sales is all about: the continual business relationship and seeing them the next time. It's about following up.

Set a date for a follow-up meeting to tell them more about your product. Find out when the appropriate time would be to get back with them. Make a note of the particular date, whether it's the next week or next month, and then leave. That will go a long way, because clients do not want you to linger on the first call. After they've known you a while, and you're there to talk about a specific project or to review some information, they know what to expect. But make the first sales call brief, leave before they ask you to leave.

Handling Rejections

Handling rejections appropriately is a sales technique that you need to be aware of. Rejections will come up. It's not the most fun, but it will happen, so handling a rejection professionally is very important. Don't get upset with the person—have ideas on how to handle rejection.

Always be nice and courteous to the person, listen to what they say, find out why you lost an order or why something went bad. Back to sales psychology: you are gathering information, so have your notepad ready to write down what they say. It may not be pleasant, but make notes so you know what caused the situation. Being prepared for problems to happen is part of your job as a professional salesperson. What's important to do is to listen, not get upset when problems occur, and take notes. Make sure you understand what the concerns are, and repeat back their concerns to the client. Then when it's appropriate, ask how you can work on the next project together, even though you had a problem on this one. Use it as an opportunity. Be the eternal optimist.

SMARTSELLING STRATEGIES: SALES TECHNIQUES

- The first step in good sales techniques is to fine-tune your skills for meeting people, and to know how to find out who the decision maker is for your product or service.
- The first person you meet may be the assistant to the decision maker; be very professional because they will report back to the one who makes the final decision.
- Make it a practice to always refer to people you are meeting by their name.
- Always have a next step planned and scheduled for each client: follow-up will give you an advantage over your competitors.
- Keep your first sales call brief, and don't try to show everything you have on this first call.
- It is important to be face to face with a client when they are ready to decide on a purchase.
- Meeting with the client in person at decision-making time will set you apart from your competitors.
- Remember to point out the benefits of a product for your client; what's in it for them is as important as the features of the product.
- If you have trouble meeting the decision maker, try to connect with the assistant and tell them you would like to show your products to them.

- Be a source of solutions for your client's problems; they will appreciate your attentiveness.
- As a salesperson, you are selling solutions, not just products and services.
- Ask new clients what you can do to earn their business.
- Always set a date for the next follow-up meeting about your product.
- Learn appropriate ways to handle rejections and how to move on to the next project.

*All coaching is, is taking a player
where he can't take himself.*
Bill McCartney

Cause something to happen.
Coach "Bear" Bryant

8. Managing Relationships

THIS CHAPTER PROVIDES A roadmap for managing your clients, for managing relationships. Getting along with your
clients, adapting to their way of working, following up,
and releasing clients are several techniques that com-
prise relationship management. Creating strong relationships will help you become more profitable in your sales
system. As you learn about developing strategic relationships with your clients, you will become a more efficient
salesperson and have more fun in your work.

A Successful First Meeting

In the previous chapter I mentioned that in the first meeting with the decision maker you should not try to sell anything. Salespeople often make the mistake of lingering
when they first meet with the decision maker; they want
to show all their catalogs and present a lot of information,
but it's usually not helpful. Think of relationship management as continuing over a long period. For the first meeting, take only five or ten percent of the most important
information or products, and give the client a couple of
points to stimulate their interest.

Whether you're an experienced salesperson or you're new at sales, you probably already know many facts about the product you're selling. Instead of overwhelming your client on the first meeting with excessive information, perhaps too much to absorb, suggest that you could talk about it in more detail at the next meeting. Stage it so you always have topics to talk about at follow-up meetings. The next time you meet, whether it's a week or a month later, give them a little more information. You'll always have a chance to come back. Don't feel that you must tell them everything you know. When you preface your meeting by saying that you need only ten or fifteen minutes of their time to tell them a few things about the product or service you sell, and that you will follow up the next time with a little more information, the client will appreciate you.

The goal for the first several meetings, especially the first meeting, is to get to know the client, so it is helpful if they do most of the talking. Ask open-ended questions so they have the opportunity to speak. You will learn about them as you're building a rapport. Taking notes emphasizes that you care about them and the notes will help you remember later what you learned. Most people in sales talk too much. I had this problem several years ago, and I've worked on it by taking notes and calming down, and letting the client speak more than I do.

Selling is not a race. Keep in mind to take your time, and know that it's a process. You're involved in a long marathon of sorts, but you are not sprinting to the finish, especially when you're selling big-ticket items. The sales process takes a long time. The client builds more trust with you as they learn more about you and your product, and you learn more about them.

While the client is talking and you think of a question, do not interrupt the client. Write down your question. When you interrupt another person, they generally lose their train of thought, or they just quit talking and shut down because they think you have heard enough. Let your client keep talking, without interrupting them. When I have a question I make a note of it and put a little circle to the left of the question. Then when I ask the question later, I put a little X through it. This way I know what I want to go back to when the person has finished speaking. But don't interrupt because the client needs time to formulate their thoughts.

Integrity

Integrity: I cannot think of anything more important in sales than integrity. I'm a straight up, honest person, and when I work with you in coaching, I will be totally honest with you. You can end up in a lot of difficulty if you lie to people. It just doesn't work out well to lie. There'll be many occasions for you to fudge the truth, but it will not help you overall; you might get an order out of it, but word will get around that you are not honest. So be honest; if a client asks you something about your product or if they ask if the product meets a certain specification and you don't know, tell them you don't know, and that you will find out the answer. Or if they ask to have their product delivered the next day and you know you can't do that, just tell them you can't do it. You might mention that the material ships from another state or another country. Be upfront with them, even if you lose that one order because they need something tomorrow, and there's no way you can deliver tomorrow. But the long-term relationship is what you're building, and they will trust you.

If you don't know the answer to a question at the moment, you can find out. Even after I've been selling floor covering for thirty-five years, people ask me technical questions I can't answer, and I must call a technical person or customer service. I get the information and then call the client back. If it's a difficult situation for me, I ask the person at the manufacturing facility to call the client. It might be easier to be the facilitator by putting the person from the manufacturing facility or at your office in touch directly with the client. There's no reason for you to be the middle-man, and it may be better to step back and let the technical person from the manufacturing facility talk to the person who has the question. The client will be pleased when the person most informed on technical details about the product provides a clear and specific answer to their question.

Integrity is crucial in long-term relationships. If you're not sure of something, take a few seconds and think about what you want to say, but don't tell a lie. Nobody is perfect, but it's important to have the highest integrity with your clients.

Delivering Information—Be Timely

Use your sales psychology: step into the client's shoes and anticipate their needs.

Always keep clients informed. Be a few steps ahead of your clients, so they don't need to call and ask when the material they ordered will be delivered, or when the service that you said you would take care of for them will happen. When will that paper be here? When will that information be here? Be proactive, so it is not necessary for the client to ask these questions; anticipate the client's needs. Be timely, whether it's good news or bad news. Every month I'm faced with delivering information to some client that is not what they want to hear: maybe their material is not arriving on time, or I won't be able to make an appointment. I text them, email them, or call and explain what has happened. Let them know you are sorry, but this is not happening the way you had planned it and that you wanted to let them know immediately. When you first tell them, they may be upset with you, but they know that nothing's perfect. They know that you are being honest and timely, and they will respect you.

Make the Purchasing Process Easy

Putting yourself in the client's shoes makes your job as a salesperson easier. The person you're working with has many things to do in a day. Make the way you deal with that client very easy for them, so they feel that the process is seamless, simple, and fun. Show the client that you, as the salesperson, are on top of everything: on top of the shipments, the delivery, everything they requested, and that you get back to them right away. This approach will encourage the person to continue a good business relationship for a long time with you. When you make it fun for them to work with you and they know that you will take care of everything right away, they can move on to other matters.

Be Brief and Efficient

Be efficient in your sales calls and know the two or three points that you want to cover. Never linger at the client's office. Don't sit around chatting casually. That might be okay when you have known somebody for several years, but in the first five to ten sales calls with the new client, don't linger. Don't leave them feeling like you took up their entire morning or afternoon!

Watch for non-verbal clues with clients; this is sales psychology. If they are looking at their watch or they seem to be daydreaming and not paying attention to you, these are all non-verbal clues and you need to respond accordingly.

Your job is to initiate each contact with a client. Occasionally the client will call you for something that they need unexpectedly, but try to be part psychologist and anticipate what that person might need. If they must call you on a regular basis to get information or ask questions, they will be annoyed. I guarantee you that they're going to be looking for a new salesperson, probably a competitor of yours, who makes their job easy. That's why you want to make their job as easy as possible.

Treat All Clients the Same

Treat all clients the same. You will have small clients and medium-sized clients and large clients. You never know when a small client could become your most important client; it might be next month or five years from now. On many occasions, someone I considered to be a small- to medium-sized client has contacted me, and suddenly I have a huge order because I stayed in touch and I treated them the same as others.

Stay in touch with each client without irritating them. Some people want to be contacted every week, others don't want to be contacted more than once a year, and you have to know their preference. I've stepped over the line many times with certain clients, and it irritates them; and sometimes they get irritated so much over a little thing that they don't want to talk to me anymore. It's their decision, and you have to accept it. Make an effort to find out how often each client would like you to contact them regarding a specific project. If they say six months from now, that's fine. I learned a long time ago that six months will be there in six months, and you'll have something to follow up on in six months. We will be more relaxed and happy as salespeople when we know we have a project to work on in the future.

Tell your clients in person that they are very important to you. Everybody wants to be important to someone else, and if you use those words and mention their name and that you appreciate every order and doing business with them, it will help in your relationship. You can't do that after the second call, or after the first order, but you can be sincere and after the first or second order thank them very much for the order. Frequently salespeople do not say please and thank you, but when you do those little things, it will be helpful for you.

Thank the client for their time as well as their business. Time is valuable, and if they give you ten minutes of their time, or an hour, to come in and meet with them, you need to thank them. Set yourself apart from other salespeople, and be a true professional. You may not remember to do this every time, but it's like a batting average. If you can get your batting average to eighty or ninety percent, that's fantastic. When you are a true professional all the time with each client and treat them with respect, it will benefit you.

Losing an Order

When you lose an order, and you will lose orders, ask the client why you lost the order. And if you can, go see the person. Don't be defensive or angry. You've already lost the order. If you can learn from a mistake you made, or you can find out why the client bought from someone else, it will help you in the future, and that's part of relationship management. Something else you can do is to say that you really appreciate the last couple of orders they placed with you, and ask how they feel about your product. Speaking of the word "feel": it is an important word versus the word "think." Feel is a sensitive emotion to people, and it's a much better word to use than "think" when you want information. Again, when you win an order, thank the client. When you lose an order, find out why, and let the client know that you want to do better—that you want to have a better chance of getting the next order from them.

Remain positive throughout this process. Sometimes it's easy to meet with someone after losing an order, but you're still upset. When you talk to the person about why you lost the order, be positive and tell them you want to do a better job, and that's why you are there. Ask them to be honest and tell you the reasons why they purchased from your competitor, and they will normally tell you.

Each client has their unique style, and it's your job to adapt to their style of working with you. Don't ever ask a client to change their style; if you know that they're always ten minutes late, that's their style. You'll be on time, and if they're late, that's fine. But you be on time; it's your job to adjust to their style. Make this fun for yourself. It's fascinating to me how some people are always ten minutes late and others are always fidgeting in their chair. I find it fascinating to learn about these different people. When you make your sales processes fun and entertaining for yourself, you will be much more efficient with what you do.

Working on your relationship management skills affects all aspects of your life. Most of us want to work on ourselves and to work on our relationships. When you work on yourself, it leads to profit. Have fun working on your relationship management skills; I want it to lead to profit for you, because we all want to make money and that's what I want you to do.

SmartSelling Strategies: Managing Relationships

- Creating strong relationships will help you become more profitable in your sales system.
- In the first meeting with the decision maker don't try to sell anything.
- Think of relationship management as continuing over a long period.

- Instead of overwhelming your client in the first meeting with excessive information, perhaps too much to absorb, suggest that you talk about it in more detail at the next meeting.
- The goal for the first several meetings is to get to know the client, so it is helpful if they do most of the talking.
- Taking notes emphasizes to the client that you care about them, and it will help you remember later what you learned.
- I cannot think of anything more important in sales than integrity.
- The client builds more trust with you when they learn more about you and you learn more about them, and when they know more about your product.
- While the client is talking and you think of a question during any presentation or meeting, do not interrupt the client; write down your question.
- Always keep clients informed; stay a few steps ahead of your clients, so they don't need call and ask when the material they ordered from you will be delivered, or when the service that you promised will happen.
- Each client has their unique style, and it's your job to adapt to their style of how they want to work with you.

Most people get excited about games, but I've got to be excited about practice, because that's my classroom.

Pat Summit, Basketball

There may be people that have more talent than you, but there's no excuse for anyone to work harder than you do.

Derek Jeter

9. Online Sales

BEING SKILLED IN ONLINE sales is an important part of sales, regardless of whether you are an online salesperson full-time or part-time, or you're an outside salesperson and you work with an online salesperson as a teammate or partner in your business. The information here pertains to both situations. Whatever you're doing in sales, it's inevitable that some portion of it will be online sales. When you develop a passion for what you're doing online, it comes through in your communication with your clients. Passion leads to fun and profit for you. My coaching, online and in person, is all about passion, fun, and profit for you.

Whether you are answering miscellaneous website inquiries for your company or you are being proactive in starting your own conversations online as a professional online salesperson, the sales techniques are similar. As a professional, try your best to be unique, to be yourself. Work to set yourself apart from everybody else that does online sales.

Communicating online is an art, and you must work at your business every day. Whether you own your own business or you are an employee of a company, it does not matter, but you must own your clients as your own business and consider them as your own clients. Either way, you're growing your own business as a professional online salesperson. Also think about related products and services that you can sell. Maybe you can constantly add new products and new services that go along with what you're already selling.

Be organized and keep track of all your clients. These are *your* clients, it is *your* business, and you will learn here how to manage that, because it's *your* responsibility to manage *your* business. Do your best to be enthusiastic—it shows that you enjoy what you're doing, and it comes across when you're communicating online with your clients. You will be the type of person the client wants. They want someone who gets excited about what they sell online.

> Concentrate on the benefits of your product and service, what's in it for your client.

There are features and benefits to every product or service. Concentrate on the benefits of your product and service, what's in it for your client. Some clients get bored if you describe too many features at one time. They are interested in what the product or service will do for them, what's in it for them. Look at it like the pitcher and the catcher in baseball or softball, as if you're the pitcher and you're giving the client a lot of information.

But think about what they catch. Put yourself in the client's shoes. There are many features and many benefits, so don't try to present all these features and benefits at one time. Work this process, and let it take its time as you get all this information out, but again, the critical thing is—what's the benefit for your client? What's in it for the client?

In our society we have numerous choices, which sometimes is a problem because people don't make choices very easily. I happen to like peanut butter, and when I go to Cost-Co to buy peanut butter, there are two choices. I buy one or the other. Cost-Co understands a customer's psychology, and they understand that if they have twenty types of peanut butter, either people won't make a decision and they'll just pass on it, or it will take too long and the person will become frustrated.

It's effective as the expert online salesperson to get to know your clients and help them narrow their choices. Help your client do what I call "try on." You can't do this in person because you're working online, but you can send samples of the product and provide information via email. Think of this as a car; the salesperson wants you to test-drive the car. Or a clothing salesperson in a retail store encourages customers to try on the clothes because they want them to fall in love with the clothing. That's what you want your client to do: to like your product and to think that they must have the product or service you're selling online.

You need to communicate online a minimum of five times with each client before they begin to trust you. They want to see if you follow up with another email and if you do what you said you would do. Most of your competitors will contact a potential client one time and won't follow up again if that client either doesn't respond or says, "No thank you." Be the person who continues to call on them at least five times so they can begin to trust you. This will be a big advantage, so be persistent with your online sales.

In addition to knowing your own products, know your competitors' products. And most importantly, know the advantages of your products over the competitors'. When clients online tell you about a competitor's product they're looking at, don't say anything negative about the competitor. Simply state, "That is a great product you're looking at, and I want you to know the advantages of the product I'm talking to you about." Then go from there, but don't mention anything negative about the competitor.

It's important to have recommendations for online sales from clients you've had for a long period. Once you get to know somebody online and they have purchased a few items from you, ask them for a letter of recommendation. There's no problem if they don't do it. Maybe they're too busy, or they look at you as a good salesperson but they don't feel comfortable writing a letter that will be seen by the public. But if some of them do write a letter, which they will, you'll be able to share these letters with your other clients.

Personally, what I do is to call satisfied clients requesting letters of recommendation. Now I have over a hundred letters. I've been in the floor covering business for thirty-five years as a manufacturer's representative. I represent companies that make flooring products, and I show these letters of recommendation to my prospects, because it gives me instant credibility. Having great letters of recommendation will do the same for you online.

To easily step into the top ten percent of successful online salespeople, have honest conversations online with your clients. Let them know you appreciate their business and tell them that you will work very hard to continue to earn their business. Also, be upfront and honest with every client, whether you have positive information or problematic information; they will respect you for this.

Set up your sales process so the client doesn't have to email or call you for information or other details. Anticipate their needs and let them know when the information will be delivered, whether it's via email or you are mailing them something. Or if something they've purchased will be delivered, let them know when they can expect to receive it. And there will be issues, and that's part of the job—our service—as salespeople, because we must take care of those problems. But the key thing is to be upfront and let the client know that an issue has come up.

Good things do come out of bad situations, so try to turn negatives into positives. When you lose an order, have an honest conversation with the person. You can apologize if necessary. Whether it's your fault or not, when you say "I'm sorry," it goes a long way with your client. And you can ask them, "How can I improve? I really want to do business with you." You turn negatives into positives by having an honest conversation with someone online.

When working online, don't attempt to tell the customer everything in one message. There may be many features and benefits to mention about your product, but a person can only absorb so much at a time, so give them a little information in several messages over time.

Treat all online clients the same, because you don't know when a small client will become a large client. Treat all clients professionally, be kind and courteous to each one, and you'll be pleasantly surprised with a client who usually buys just a small amount every year from you. That client may suddenly place a big order because you have done such a great job with your online communication.

The words "please" and "thank you" are so powerful. You need to use these words online and in phone calls to your clients. These words really count and clients appreciate hearing them. Make a big point of saying, "Please may I get this information for you, and thank you for communicating with me, thank you very much for your business."

Tracking Your Online Business

I use a mental, or visualization, method to keep track of all my projects in my head. Refer also to chapter two, Organization and Time Management, for more detail about this process. I visualize what I call "the tube." Visualize or imagine a tube that goes on for a mile. Clients and projects that you're working on go into the tube at one end and come out at the other end to become an order. When a project gets through "the tube," it is an order.

Understand that this is a mental process, not something to write down. In the sales process, someone contacts you, you contact them through email, and they're interested in your product. Information about the customer goes into your mental tube. You provide information and maybe send them a sample, and in your system they keep working their way through the tube until they order something from you.

Many things can happen. People shop online, communicate with you and other online salespeople, and they gather information. You talk to them, and then it stops, and maybe they don't decide for a multitude of reasons. But they're still right there and your job as the professional online salesperson is to figure out how to get them from there to the purchase. For example, find out when they want you to follow up next. They may say that they're going on a trip, or they don't have the money right now. That's okay. They're not giving you a no, so they're still in the tube. It helps you relax, knowing there are many projects and clients in the tube.

It's very important to respond to clients ASAP. I have won many projects in my long sales career because people tell me, "Eddy, I contacted three sales reps, and you're the only one who got back to me within a couple hours. Some of them didn't get back to me for a couple days." In this fast-paced world we live in, ASAP is very important, so don't wait too long. You will improve your sales by getting back to the client right away.

Constantly reprioritize your schedule based on what is happening in the moment. Urgent matters move to the top of the list, and therefore as an online salesperson don't over-schedule, because people will contact you online and want information immediately. Take breaks in your schedule so that you can take care of those needs right away—don't be the kind of salesperson who gets to it tomorrow or the next day. When someone contacts you, be proactive and get right back to them.

I happen to use the **A-B-C** method for keeping track of clients. In this system, **A** includes the most important clients. The **B** and **C** clients I want to move up to the **A** list, but I focus every day on the **A** clients. They are bringing me the business. This type of list will help you know where to focus your attention. The **A-B-C** list is explained in more detail in chapter two.

Being organized in online sales will equal success and fun, and disorganization equals frustration and burnout. These feelings are not helpful for anyone. When you're organized and you know what you're doing the next day or next week as a professional online salesperson, you will feel much better about your whole life. It feels good to be organized and it will help you relax. I relax when I know what I will be doing and what I'm working on. Otherwise, sales can be very stressful. Online sales, every kind of sales, can be stressful, so it's helpful to find ways to limit our stress.

Ask your client how you can help with anything related to their recent purchase. You are an online salesperson forever with this person. Keep communication open with them until they're ready to make the next purchase. You will step up to the top ten percent of online salespeople by being proactive and following up after the sale. Send a message and ask, "What can I do to make this purchase even better for you? I really appreciate your buying from me, and I want to know what else I can do now to make you happier or to answer any questions." Assume that there's something about the purchase they just made with you that can be improved.

Be prepared for problems and handle them professionally. Handling rejection: there will be rejection—it will happen. People will reject you. But remember to be polite and respectful online, because it might create an opportunity to work with them later.

Work to continually add new projects and prospects to your list so that you always have more projects to work on. Don't do this so fast that you become overwhelmed; you will feel stress and burnout. But as you are able, add more projects and more clients. Also ask for referrals from your happy clients, because they like what you do and they will refer you to other people.

It will be helpful to you if you can be a source of solutions to problems. People may go online and communicate with you because they have a problem they need to solve. Be a resource, not just a salesperson. You're the professional in your area, whatever the product or service is that you sell online, and the odds are ninety-nine percent that you know more than the person contacting you. Be a resource for them and answer all their concerns; think about making their problems go away. They will most likely come back to you for a purchase.

You call customer service or you chat with someone online when you want help. That's exactly what these people want from you. Clients want to work with people who solve their problems; it's that simple. They have an issue. They need something for their computer, they need a special tool, they need a new bike. Whatever it is you sell online, they want a solution, so sell solutions. Clients and prospects will appreciate your service.

To be great at online sales, constantly work on improving your skills. Take advantage of the many free online resources to help improve your skills with online communication, particularly with marketing. You might enjoy my webinars, too!

SMARTSELLING STRATEGIES: ONLINE SALES

- Be yourself and be unique when you work online; communicating online is an art.
- Consider all your clients to be your own clients, even if you work for a company.
- When presenting your products online, emphasize the benefits for the client.
- Help people narrow their choices from the numerous options available online.
- Plan to communicate with each potential online client at least five times so they will begin to trust you.
- Follow up online when you say you will follow up.
- Familiarize yourself with the products your competitors are selling online.
- Ask for letters of recommendation from online clients after you have worked with them on several projects.
- Be timely in responding to clients so they don't need to email you or call you with questions.
- When an issue comes up, be honest and tell the client there is a problem.
- Treat all online clients with the same respect and attention.
- Use the words "please" and "thank you" in your emails.

- When you work online, be able to adjust and reprioritize your schedule to respond quickly to clients with requests or issues.
- Know how to handle rejection politely and appropriately online.
- Be an online source of solutions for your clients.

I do not know of any single soul who succeeded in life without a mentorship.
Lailah Gifty Akita

A good coach asks great questions to help you remove the obstacles in your mind and to get you back on track in life.
Farshad Asi

10. Retail Sales and Inside Sales

Building Relationships

THIS CHAPTER IS PARTICULARLY for retail salespeople and inside salespeople; the strategies for success are quite similar in both situations. In the case of inside salespeople, some will handle only incoming calls, while others will also make outgoing calls. I have frequently worked as a teammate with inside salespeople. Often the inside salesperson is not only the inside contact but will also do follow-up work with the same customers. Inside salespeople are crucial to every outside salesperson because as the inside contact they provide important information.

I also have quite a bit of experience with retail sales. I grew up in the retail business in Kansas City. My parents had women's clothing stores. At a very young age, I learned about retail sales when I was unboxing dresses and all kinds of clothes and steaming the clothing to make it presentable to the customer. So retail business has always been part of my life. My parents showed me that the business was all about the relationships with customers. This is very important, because you are building relationships over many years with your clients. I've been in the retail flooring business, calling on retail flooring stores, for many years. Over a thirty-five-year period, my business has been representing manufacturers that make all kinds of flooring products. I've visited many retail stores in the flooring business over those thirty-five years.

As an inside salesperson, building a relationship with each customer is crucial to being successful. Building a business relationship doesn't happen in one day or one week. Constantly work on building your client relationships. Once you've built a relationship, doing what it takes to maintain the friendship is also essential. One of the essential aspects of building the business relationship is to make great notes when someone gives you information and to have thorough records. My goal is to help you get into the top ten percent of all inside salespeople. To do this, you need to keep good records on your clients in order to build a database.

Most retail salespeople simply wait for a client, which is not the best approach for success in sales. This book provides you with information and skills to help you get into the top ten percent of all retail salespeople in your field. To get to the top five percent or the top one percent, you have to work on your own, and I can help you as a coach or consultant. It's not about waiting for your clients; you need to be proactive and manage your business. Whether you own your own store or you work at a retail store, it really doesn't matter. Either way, look at your business as if you are managing your own business. This approach will equal profit for you.

Habits of likeable people:
They lose the power pose;
They embrace the power of touch;
They allow the other person to talk about
theirself without the other person ever
knowing it happened;
Being a great listener makes you very
likeable;
They let the other person be better than
they are. Don't try to "one up" them;
Likeable people focus on what they can do
for others;
Close your meetings with sincerity; "I'm
really glad I met you" makes a lasting
impression.

Keeping Records, Being Organized

To manage your business so it grows, you need to do several things. First, keep detailed records. Organization and follow-up are two of the most important assets for both inside salespeople and retail salespeople. You need to keep track of your clients and get to know them as much as possible. Know what they like, know when their birthdays are, know their anniversary if they are married, know about their children and their animals. The more you know, it helps you build a relationship and the better you're going to do.

Both inside salespeople and retail salespeople need to inform your clients when new products are coming in. Know a client's history of what they like to buy from you. Let them know about pre-sales. When products are coming in, send an email or a mailer to inform them. If you are in retail sales, find creative ways to get your clients into the store. Be proactive to get them in: talk to them on the phone and keep a dialogue going with them. The same is true for inside salespeople. Send discount cards to clients, letting them know that because they are a preferred customer, they will get discounts from you.

When you love what you do, it really shows. I love sales coaching because I have a lot of experience, and I want you to become fantastic—make more money, have more passion, have more fun with your sales process. Laugh and smile with your clients. Clients like a retail salesperson they can work with on a regular basis and who really gets to know them. You can set yourself apart from ninety percent of your competitors, if you do these few things: be proactive and work on your relationships with your customers.

Sales Psychology

To be great at retail sales and inside sales, you need to love people and want to understand the other person. Sales is all about psychology. First, you must understand yourself. In order to understand others, you first must learn about yourself, because we all have things that we need to work on. So first learn to understand your own psychology and then start learning about your clients. You must adapt to your clients; changing someone else is almost impossible. Your clients are the way they are, and you take them for what they are; you as the salesperson must adapt to them. The only thing you can do is to work on yourself and then adapt to their style.

Pay attention to the client. Is the client paying attention to you? The only way you know that is by paying attention to them. Listen to how they speak to you on the phone, their tone of voice, and hear how fast they are speaking. If you are with them, watch their facial expressions and their body movements. For example, if you have a product that has a hundred features and you're reviewing all the features, most likely you will bore the person, unless they're very technical or they want to know every detail about how something is made. That's a very rare individual. Mention the high points; know the two or three main features about your product or service that you're selling at the retail level. Then watch your client and see what they do; watch their facial expressions and their body movements and see if they're starting to fall asleep. If they are bored, back off. If you are working online, be aware of the tone of their messages and the language they use.

Most people want a salesperson who is enthusiastic and likes what they do, and who really wants to help the customer. But sometimes salespeople get too excited or too enthusiastic about what we do. You might wonder how that can be a problem. Sometimes it can backfire if you get overly excited about what you sell. But if you happen to annoy a customer, find out what the problem is and then try to work on it. For example, if you are working with someone who is a quiet person, try to speak more softly or slowly. The key point about enthusiasm is that for every sale you lose because you are too enthusiastic, you'll lose a hundred if you are not enthusiastic enough.

The Sales Pitch

Practice your sales pitch in the mirror, whether you are an inside salesperson or in retail sales. Practice a sales pitch on selling something you have in your retail store. It will really help you. You'll see your facial movements, you'll see how much you smile; those things are important. Even on the phone, smiling is critical. People can tell when you're on the phone if you're smiling and having fun, or not. Work on smiling when you're listening to them when you are on the phone or when they're in your store. And use the client's name because they appreciate that. All these practices will help you have a better business relationship with your clients.

Inside salespeople will be talking on the phone but also emailing and sending out other types of communications. Practice writing in a style that is suitable for online communication. There are many resources online about blogging and writing for the internet. Your passion will come across in your email messages.

To improve yourself and your skills, talk to friends and your best clients and get advice on how you can become better. Feel free to ask for constructive criticism. Say to them honestly, "I would like to do a better job working with you, and if you would tell me how I could improve, I really would appreciate that." Listen and write down what they say, so you will know what to work on.

Listening Well

Good listeners in our society are very well liked. It's an interesting phenomenon; when people talk about themselves, they like you. I've been to many parties, and I've learned over the years to ask open-ended questions about the person I'm speaking with. I also do this when I want to get to know clients or friends better. With clients, I have a pad of paper and a pen, and I listen very carefully and take notes. I've had many interviews for the purpose of getting to know the person and they want to get to know me. So we set up an hour meeting, and they spend the entire time talking about theirself. That's fine, because we can get together again for coffee or lunch. But at the end of the conversation these people tell me, "Oh wow, I had so much fun talking to you," and I just smile because I know they did all the talking. Psychologically, they like you. Keep that in mind.

We have two ears and one mouth, so when you're on the phone as an inside salesperson, listen twice as much as you talk. It's all about the client. When you're learning about the client, you're getting to know them and how they purchase, and what types of things they have bought in the past. And when you are a good salesperson you will learn about their family, their children, their animals, and vacations they've been on. They will begin to trust you and talk to you about personal matters. But don't interrupt and start talking about yourself. It's all about the client, so listen carefully and take good notes because your job is to create a database. You're gathering information about each client; the more you can write down about them, the better it is.

Communication is not just what we say. These are informative statistics: fifty-five percent of all communication is non-verbal; thirty-eight percent is our tone of voice; only seven percent of what we convey is content, the words that come out. So again: fifty-five percent, nonverbal; thirty-eight percent, tone; and seven percent, content. Remember this, because it's very useful for your presentations.

Pay attention to the tone of your voice when you talk with clients. How much you smile, your body movements, all these habits are very important to notice. Years back, I had the habit of clicking my pen due to being nervous. But when you are with clients and friends, these habits probably annoy them. This is where coaching can be very helpful. You as a retail salesperson oftentimes cannot see what you're doing wrong yourself. It's just like pro-athletes, who all have coaches because they can't see what they're doing wrong. Have friends or family members help you with this; find out what you do that bothers them and they'll be honest with you. Write down their points and work on them.

What's in It for the Client: the Benefits

Features and benefits are a high priority for anyone making a purchase, whether it is personal or for a business. It's important for inside salespeople and retail salespeople to find a balance between talking about features and talking about benefits of a product. Many salespeople talk mostly about the features of the product. But features are just one aspect of what you're promoting. State the features of the product and then explain how these features will benefit your customer. The significant attraction you need to promote is the benefit. The benefit means what's in it for them. It's important to present the benefits, and you need to focus on benefits. Yes, state some or all of the features, depending on what you're selling, but emphasize the benefits to your client. Find out what the customer is most interested in and talk about the benefits of that; they want to hear the benefits. It's all about the client and what interests them, and what positive impact the product would have for them.

As an inside salesperson, find creative ways to help your client "try on" the product, as mentioned earlier. Even though you're working as an inside salesperson, you can send out samples of whatever you sell or send literature by email, so the customer has more information. But if they can touch the product, that's even better. It's great when clients fall in love with the products you sell, just as if they were trying on clothes in a store or test-driving a car. This is fundamental for being a successful inside salesperson, when face-to-face contact doesn't occur.

Demonstrations make a strong impression; as mentioned earlier, a presentation without a demonstration is just a conversation. In a demonstration you will be doing something, and you can get the client involved. Take retail sales, using clothing as an example. If you're selling a scarf to a customer, get them involved in the demonstration by inviting them to put on the scarf. Let the customer "try on" the product, and they will become more interested.

Choices

Help the client narrow down their choices. Whatever you are selling at the retail level, there are many choices, and the customer frequently gets overwhelmed. Your job is to show the client mainly the products you think they are most interested in. You must know your products inside and out; for all the products that you sell know as much detail as you can. Most of the time you won't use all the information with your client, but it's very important to learn as much as you can about your specific products.

As an excellent inside salesperson, get to know your client so well that you will be able to help them narrow down their choices. Then, for whatever product or service you're selling, make it easy for your client to acknowledge the benefits of the product. If you have products that are very expensive, all the way down to commodity-type products, and you find out that a client only wants the best of whatever you sell, don't waste your time and their time talking about the commodity products, because that's not what they want. They want the best products, and that's what you need to know as the inside salesperson to be able to make the sale.

It's also important to know your competitors' products because most people shop around. Understand the advantages of your product over the competition. You also must know the features and benefits of the competitors' products, but never speak negatively about the competitors. When someone comes in and says they are looking for a scarf, for a bike, or whatever you're selling, and they tell you that they have seen a particular product at another store, just say, "That's great and it's a really good product, and I want to tell you the advantages of the products that I have to sell you," and go from there, but don't ever speak negatively about your competitors—it doesn't do you any good.

Asking for the Order

At the retail level it is important to know when to ask for the order. Just before you ask, find out what additional questions the client might have regarding the product they are considering. Let the client know that you have reviewed everything with them. Immediately before you ask for the order, do not speak, even if it is difficult not to; give the client a chance to talk. You are encouraging them to say, "I don't have any other questions and I think you've answered everything." At that point, ask the client if they are ready for you to write up their order, or if they are ready to make a deposit, or whatever the next step is, and then calmly pause to see what they say.

Listen to your client without the intent to respond. In our society, almost everybody interrupts. Try listening without interrupting, and just take notes so that you can learn about your client. Use the words "Tell me…" because the client will offer more information with an open-ended question and you will learn more.

Being Honest

Be upfront and honest with your client, always, with everything that you're promoting and selling at the retail level or as an inside salesperson. The client will respect you for having the highest integrity. If you don't know the answer to something, find out and get back to the client. Take, for example, the delivery of a product. If you have told a client that a delivery is scheduled in a couple of weeks and then you find out that it will be late, inform the client immediately. It may not be your fault. Maybe the factory where the material ships from is late. Just tell the client. They may get a little upset, but they know that it's out of your control. Be proactive and inform the client before the delivery date becomes an issue and they need to call you.

Always keep the client informed on the good and the bad. Let them know what is happening. Get inside their brain, use your psychology, and let them know the important details such as the delivery date or information they may want on the product or the service that you're selling at the retail level. A professional salesperson must anticipate the client's needs.

Have a sense of humor, laugh at yourself; it's very important to be able to laugh at yourself—we all make mistakes. It's okay to laugh. Smile and have fun with your clients, have fun at your job, have passion, and it will lead to profit for you at the retail level.

Treat All Clients the Same

Treat all clients the same. I've learned this over and over again. I have started with some small clients, and a few years later suddenly they place a huge order. As a retail salesperson you never know where a big order will come from. Somebody might come in regularly and buy something small from you, but they might become a very significant client for you by placing a huge order. This is the benefit of treating all clients the same.

"Please" and "Thank you"—I want to emphasize how important this is. I deal with salespeople and I coach salespeople all the time who literally don't say please and thank you. Someone may place an order when I'm on a sales call with a salesperson, coaching them at the retail level, and that retail salesperson doesn't say thank you. It's essential to say please and thank you to your customers. These courtesies really count; the clients appreciate your attention and are totally cognizant of this.

Being Organized

Filing systems! Have a system to keep up with all your clients. Especially if you are a new salesperson, you will continue to get more and more clients. I have a very simple two-tier file system, which is explained in detail in chapter two. I write down important information on a piece of paper. The critical thing is that you have a system to be organized and that you follow up with all your clients. In addition to written notes on each client, I always have a follow-up date for each client. So even if they haven't bought anything for a while, I have a follow-up date and maybe I'll be in contact with them quarterly, either calling them or sending an email.

A salesperson who wants to get in the top ten percent must be organized and follow up. In my own system, if there's a project I need to follow up within the month, I put a note in the top file. If the follow-up is the next month or later, it could be a year from now, it goes in the bottom file. At the end of every week I go through the top file and prioritize the projects, so I know what I will be doing in the coming week. At the end of every month I go through the bottom file and move anything requiring attention in the coming month to the top file.

Good organization is crucial and it leads to success and fun for you. If you're disorganized, you will be frustrated because you don't know what to do next, and it turns into burnout. For example, you may forget to follow up with a client to let them know when their delivery is coming in. The client will then need to call you. Organization and timely response are essential to your success.

Remember to ask a client how you can help with anything related to their recent purchase. You are a salesperson from the moment someone walks into your store and becomes a client and you learn their name. They will be your client hopefully for a long time. You will sell them a product, then arrange for delivery of the product if it's something that will be shipped later, and then follow up with them after they have received the product. Call and thank them for their purchase and find out what you can do to help with anything related to the purchase.

Be timely and ask your clients what you could do to make their purchase experience better for them. Take the example of going out to dinner. The server or host will come up to you after you've had your meal and ask if everything was okay. They should have asked you during the meal. Probably ninety-nine out of a hundred people will say yes, regardless of whether the meal was terrible or not. At that point there's nothing to talk about, it's just a formality. With your client, you might say, "How can I help you with what you just purchased from me?" With this approach, just asking what would have made it more fun or pleasant is good for your relationship.

Constantly be adding new prospects to call on. When you're a great retail salesperson, you have a certain number of clients. Ask the best clients for referrals to add to your database. Add more clients to work with, and start the ball rolling to get them to be your customers. I group clients into **A**, **B**, and **C** clients. I suggest you try a similar system. The **A** clients will be the source of eighty percent of your income, but don't discount the **B** and **C** clients. Get the **B** and **C** clients to move up, if possible. But your primary focus is with the **A** clients because they like you and you like them. For me, the real difference between an **A** client and other clients is that there is mutual respect, and I find that this is really important. You work well together, and the **A** client is somebody who appreciates what you do as an outstanding retail salesperson.

Always ask clients for referrals because you want your database to grow. But don't get so many clients at one time that you can't handle all of them. Routinely talk to your clients about referrals because you want to add these people to your database. Invite them to bring their friends into your store if they can, or offer to contact their friends via phone or email.

Talk to friends and family. Often friends and family don't really understand what you do, except in a very general way. But let your friends and family know what you do, maybe chat with them at a family gathering or meet for coffee and let them know in a very detailed way what you do at the retail level. Tell them what kind of customers you are looking for and ask for suggestions.

In retail sales you are a source of solutions to people's problems. People come to your store to purchase products to help them in some way. Sometimes people buy things simply to feel happy. So be a resource to them, not just a salesperson. Most salespeople just wait on the sales floor for somebody to come in. You will be in the top ten percent when you are proactive. Be a resource to these people, and own your own business even if you don't own the company; manage your customers, and you will do very well in retail sales.

Work regularly on your skills. We all have something we need to work on, and you can have fun with this. Write down the things that you're good at, write down whatever you need to improve on. We all have things to work on. Make this fun for yourself as you become an outstanding salesperson.

SMARTSELLLING STRATEGIES: RETAIL SALES AND INSIDE SALES

- When you are an inside salesperson, practice treating your clients as if you were seeing them in person.
- Building relationships with your clients is essential to your success.
- Practice smiling when you are speaking on the phone; your client will know you are smiling.
- Use the client's name whenever you can.
- Remember to emphasize the benefits of your products, as well as the features.
- Focus on building long-term relationships with your clients by understanding what they like to buy.
- Keep detailed records on each client and what they purchase from you.
- Offer occasional discounts to your clients.
- Practice your sales pitch looking in a mirror, and you will become more comfortable talking with customers.

- A presentation without a demonstration is just a conversation.
- Help the client narrow down their choices.
- Know when to ask for the customer's order.
- Learn to listen without the intent to respond, without interrupting
- Adapt your way of working to the client's style of working.
- Follow up with whatever you say you will do.
- Always find out if you can do anything for the client once they receive their product.
- Treat all clients with the same respect.
- As a retail salesperson, sell solutions for your client's problems.

*Fear is our biggest challenge.
Fear keeps us from focusing on
what we want.*

*People do not buy 'what you
do.' They buy 'why you do it!'*
Eddy Mindlin

11. Selling with Passion

I GET VERY EXCITED about sharing my passion for my work. I love what I do, and I know this has been a significant reason why I've been successful over many years. Learn to empower yourself with passion, so that you freely convey your passion to your client—passion is contagious. When you're excited about what you do, most of your clients will be excited. It will really help your sales career.

Life feels good when you love what you do. I love sales coaching and consulting because I have many good ideas to share. I've learned the art of sales as a sort of "street fighter." I've been on the streets making cold calls, being knocked down, and getting up over and over again. And, I've been doing it for thirty-five years. I relate to the problems and successes that you experience daily. That's why I want you to be passionate about what you do.

You need to love what you do with the product you're selling or whatever service you're providing to your clients. It's good to enjoy your sales calls and to appreciate each person you see in a day. Hopefully you enthusiastically say, "I get to see three people today!" instead of feeling like these visits are a chore. These are friends—business friends. You will learn about other people. Have fun while you're with clients and smile. Let your client know that you're enjoying the conversation and what they have to say to you. Enjoy presenting your product or your service to them. The enthusiasm will be contagious, and they will see that you're excited about your product. They will pay much more attention.

Love learning about your client. I don't mean super-ficially, but truly listen to him or her, and have a sincere interest in each of your clients. Everybody has something new to tell you, and everyone has different stories about what they've done in their life, their family, where they went to school, sports, arts. The more you learn about your client, the more comfortable the two of you will be when you are together. So again, you really need to listen. Taking notes is important, because it makes you pay attention and you can refer to those notes later. Over time, get to know as much about each client as possible.

I happen to love animals and sports, and I love children, too. For many of my best clients I know the names of their children, where they go to school, and I can tell you about their family pets because I truly care about these people. It's wonderful to be able to talk about these personal things. They all know what you're there for. You are there to sell your product or service, but you are building a lasting business relationship with these people. It shows a lot of passion by getting to know them; it's all about the client.

Being enthusiastic shows your clients that you are having fun with what you're doing. Clients want to work with a person who's excited about their product and who knows their product. When you are excited, your client will get excited. They will want to do business with you, and that's really what it's all about.

Tell the clients that you will work hard to earn their business. Use the phrase "earn their business," because nothing is given in this world. You have to earn and work hard for that business, especially the first few orders. Once you develop a good rapport with a client, you won't have to work as hard, but you'll still have to work, and you can never let down because there's always competition, always other salespeople wanting to get your business with that client. For every order, every project, you need to earn the business with them, and then you must do what you say you will do. Performing is what it's all about. Many salespeople will say, "Yes! I will do this. I'm going to do that. I will get you this information," and then they don't do it. When you say, "I will get you this information by tomorrow," do it! Do whatever you tell your client you're going to do, because they are expecting you to follow through.

Sales psychology relates to every sales strategy in our minds. Psychology is everything in sales, and it is essential to observe your client to know the best way to be with them. For example, on occasion I've been too excited about a project or about the product I sell, and I happen to be dealing with someone who is not an enthusiastic person. They're a very calm person, very quiet, don't talk too much, and so my enthusiasm has hurt me sometimes. Be aware of that, but most of the time the enthusiasm is contagious and good.

Each time you're talking, each time you're giving a presentation, be aware of the type of person your client is. Sometimes you must gear up for a specific client and sometimes you should tone it down. You may also need to speak more slowly. But you can still be enthusiastic when you're talking slowly or softly. Talk to friends and clients and get advice on improving yourself in all aspects of selling, as well as your enthusiasm level and your passion level. You want to make sure that your passion is coming across to your clients, so ask your friends about this. Write down whatever they tell you, and be willing to work on that.

Features and benefits are very important, but they're very different. The features are the specific items or details that a product has on it, for example, a car. We all know a little bit about cars. It could have a tilt steering wheel, an AM/FM radio, or adjustable seats; those are features. The benefit is what's in it for the client. The client may not care that it has a radio, it is not important to them. They may not care that the wheel is a tilt steering wheel. But for each feature mention a benefit and explain the benefit to the client. Again, the benefit is really the most important consideration.

A presentation without a demonstration is just a conversation. I always use a demonstration in my presentations because it helps people remember. When I'm giving a talk to a group of people, I'll stop for a second, then I juggle because I'm a juggler. When I juggle, I talk about juggling because juggling has everything to do with life and everything to do with sales. After I juggle for five or ten seconds, I'll stop and say, "None of you have fallen asleep yet," and of course everybody laughs, that's number one! A demonstration holds the attention of the audience; think of something in your business that you could use as a demonstration. People stay awake during your presentation because they see you doing something.

Sometimes big crowds attend my talks, and I'll say, "Who knows how to juggle?" Then I select someone who didn't raise their hand even though I'm putting him on the spot, but I can teach almost anybody to juggle. If they don't know how to juggle, I'll throw one tennis ball and say, "Throw that from your left hand to your right hand," and they are involved. When you get another person involved in your demonstration, your presentation will have a greater impact.

Encourage people to touch the product you're selling. If you're using a flip chart, it is your demonstration in the moment. But if they touch something, they are more likely to pay attention and remember that. Think about how it is for you. If you're sitting in a presentation and someone is talking to you and doing a demonstration, and they let you touch the chair or whatever it is they are selling, you remember it. People like to touch and be involved in the presentation, and it makes you a better salesperson. Whenever you can, link the demonstration to the benefit of the product or service that you're selling. This will help the client to narrow their choices.

Another way to help your client is to invite them to "try on" the product: try on a dress, try on a jacket, test-drive a car. Why do you think salespeople want you to test-drive a car? Because then you start to fall in love with the car. You start to like it. When a woman tries on a dress or shoes, or a man tries on a jacket, the salesperson will say, "Well, you look great in that," and you get excited when the salesperson shows enthusiasm. Learn how to inspire your client to get excited about what you're selling.

After your client sees you a minimum of five times, they will gain trust in you. Trust is everything in sales. The client wants to trust you one hundred percent. They want to know that you're honest, that you do what you say you're going to do, and you show up when you say you will show up. See your client repeatedly; most salespeople don't. It's a big advantage for you to call on someone multiple times in order to build trust.

Know your products inside and out. If you don't know the answer to a client's question, call a technical person at your company or ask your boss or another salesperson, but always get back to the client. You need to know enough about your products to answer the ten most common questions. Whatever you're selling, there are always five to ten questions that everyone will ask, and those are the questions that you need to be prepared for.

Knowing your competition and their products is very important. What is better about your product? What is better about the competitor's product? You need to know your competitor's products so you can be prepared to answer questions and discuss your competitor's products in a nice way.

In sales, if you are unique and creative when you call on a client, you make yourself memorable. Demonstrations were mentioned earlier in this chapter. You can also find specialty marketing items like pens or key rings, little trinkets. These might cost fifty cents, but giving somebody something makes an impact. Think about what you can do in your business to make yourself memorable to your clients. I have had success with specialty marketing items, because people love to get things, and marketing trinkets are great icebreakers, too. When I go to see somebody for the first time, I give them a gift. It doesn't matter whether it's valued at fifty cents or two dollars. You're giving them something, and they say, "Wow! That's nice. Thank you." That's an icebreaker.

Sometimes I give a presentation to one person, or three or four people, and I only talk for ten or fifteen minutes. The goal is to get in somebody's office with a few specific items, and then get out. At the end, I'll give them a present and I'll say, half-jokingly, "You know I am giving you this present because you spent ten minutes with a salesperson, and thank you very much." Because a lot of them don't like to spend time with salespeople, you're thanking them for spending time with you.

Know when to ask for the order. After you've met with a customer several times, know when it's time for them to order. Don't be bashful to say, "Is there anything else I can answer for you about my product?" and if they say, "No, I think I've got everything I need to know," then just say, "Okay! I'm ready for you to place your order. When will you be ready to place your order?" and see what they have to say. It's time for them to place the order—don't be bashful with this.

Make time to network with other professionals who sell products to your clients, products that don't compete with yours. I've done this for a long time. I'm in the floor covering business, and I have good friends who sell wall covering products and furniture, for example. I meet them on a regular basis, because we call on the same people. I'm getting to know my fellow salespeople who sell other products, and we brainstorm together about how to best work on specific projects or with specific clients. Doing this will help you because you can share honest information with them since you're not competing with them, but you're working with the same clients. If you bump into a roadblock with certain clients, you can go to your peers who sell other products to them and ask for advice, which can be very helpful.

Never speak poorly about your competitors. The best thing you can do when people say something negative is to say nothing. Or say something like, "That's really a good product," or "That person is a nice salesperson." Obviously, they know you're there to sell your product, so don't get into deep water, because that can give you a bad reputation of talking poorly about your competitors. And there's nothing wrong with making nice comments about your competitors. Many times I've taken the opportunity to say, "Yeah, I'm familiar with that salesperson, and they're a great salesperson and the product line they represent is wonderful. However, here's how I can offer you a better product or better service or better pricing." Then talk about the benefits of what you have to sell as opposed to anything negative about someone else.

Letters of recommendation are critical. When you ask for a letter of recommendation, you are asking someone else to do something for you to help you. They have two choices: either "Yes I'll write a letter for you," or "No, I won't." Or they may say, "I'll do it," and they never do it. If the person takes the time and energy to spend twenty minutes writing a letter and to send it to you, they care about you. That's a strong message, because you'll quickly find out who your best allies are. Use those letters wisely and accumulate as many as you can; try to have your clients write you a letter of recommendation when you finish a project or after you have known someone over a period of a couple of years.

Some of these people will ask you to write the letter. They'll ask you to send a draft and then they may amend it and put it on their letterhead. The letter could be two sentences or twenty sentences, it doesn't matter. It must be on their letterhead with their signature, stating that you are a good salesperson, that you follow up, you're organized, and that you know your product. It will go a long way when you're showing these letters of recommendation to other people, and you feel good to have those letters of recommendation. I have over a hundred letters from many years, and I feel good about my service to my clients because I know that over a hundred people have taken the time and energy to do this.

Also, it may improve your relationship even more with the person who wrote the letter for you, when you mention that you showed the letter of recommendation to a new client, and then you thank them again for the letter. These clients really care about you. Then always show new prospects these letters of recommendation.

Live your passion in your work and improve your presentation skills. Your passion will come across to your clients, and when you have fun and you're passionate about what you do, you will make money.

SMARTSELLING STRATEGIES: SELLING WITH PASSION

- Empower yourself as a salesperson with your passion for what you do.
- Learn as much as you can about your clients because they are your business friends.

- Be sure to follow through with whatever you say you will do for a client.
- Adjust your style so that a client is comfortable with you.
- When you do a demonstration during your product presentations, a client will remember you and the products you are selling.
- Visit your client five times so they will begin to trust you.
- Network with other people who sell different products to your clients; you both will learn about dealing with a particular client.
- Avoid speaking negatively about your competitors.
- Passion is contagious, and most of your clients will appreciate your enthusiasm.

About the Author

An accomplished Independent Sales Representative for over thirty-five years, Eddy Mindlin has cultivated a reputation for integrity and accountability, and has developed a unique system for sales success—SmartSelling Strategies.

After graduating from Trinity University, Eddy began his sales career with Bigelow Carpet Mills. Just three years later he became the youngest winner of the President's Award for top sales in the company. In 1988 he launched his own business representing many floor covering lines, as well as other products needed by his clients. As he worked with architects, designers, construction companies and facilities managers Eddy perfected his distinctive approach to sales management.

Today, as a celebrated and gifted sales expert, coach, author, and speaker, Eddy inspires others to reach for their goals and ambitions.

You can learn more about Eddy and his approach by visiting www.EddyMindlin.com.

Five Reasons to Work with Me as Your Sales Coach

IF YOU'RE A SALESPERSON, sales manager, or owner of a company and want to increase your sales and have all your salespeople have more fun, I invite you to consider working with me. I will help you improve your business results and increase the personal satisfaction you enjoy by creating a successful career in sales. Some of the benefits of using me as an ongoing coach include:

1. **Experience**—After thirty-five years of selling a variety of products, I know the issues you are facing. I have had the same challenges you have, and I understand how to overcome them. I am easy and fun to work with.

2. **Hands on, not theory**—Many coaches like to share checklists, marketing philosophy, canned responses, and concepts that sound good, but don't always work in the field when you're in front of a prospect. I don't use this approach. When I work with an individual or group, we focus on the skills you need to take your career to the next level. Many times I'll go into the field with you and make sales calls. While "classroom" training is valuable, I get involved in assisting each of my clients with the specific things that apply to them.

3. **Flexible, responsive**—I don't come to you with a preconceived idea of what you need. Instead, we start with my seeking to understand where you and your team are right now, and what challenges you face. Then we work together to design steps to help you become more successful, and enjoy the process of selling.

4. **Systems**—I believe that successful sales professionals have systems to help manage their business.

Whether manual or computer based, you must have a way to track your prospects, clients, and projects throughout the sales cycle and beyond. I will help you develop this level of organization. Together we will create a system that you like and will use on a daily basis.

5. **Affordable**—I want to be accessible to the individual salesperson trying to build their career, as well as the young company developing a sales team. I don't want money to be an obstacle to our working together, so my pricing is fair and affordable.

The same passion that I channeled into building a successful sales career for myself, I now use to help other sales professionals develop their skills and enjoyment in this exciting vocation. Let's talk about how we can work together. My direct phone number is 505-269-1799. Unless I'm with a client, I even answer my own phone!